Corpse

CW01582360

For my family – the one I was born into,
and the one I found along the way.

This edition published in 2024. First published in the UK in 2022 as "The Girl, the Ghost and the Lost Name" by Usborne Publishing Limited, Usborne House, 83-85 Saffron Hill, London EC1N 8RT, England. usborne.com

Usborne Verlag, Usborne Publishing Ltd., Prüfeninger Str. 20, 93049 Regensburg, Deutschland, VK Nr. 17560

Text copyright © Reece Carter 2022

Cover illustration by Maxine Lee-Mackie © Usborne Publishing, 2024

Inside illustrations by Eleonora Asparuhova © Usborne Publishing, 2022

Title lettering © Kristy Lund-White

Additional lettering by Sarah Coleman © Usborne Publishing, 2022

Author photo © Simon Fitzpatrick

The right of Reece Carter to be identified as the author of this work has been asserted by him in accordance with the Copyright, Designs and Patents Act, 1988.

The name Usborne and the Balloon logo are Trade Marks of Usborne Publishing Ltd.

All rights reserved. No part of this publication may be reproduced, stored in a retrieval system or transmitted in any form or by any means without the prior permission of the publisher.

This is a work of fiction. The characters, incidents, and dialogues are products of the author's imagination and are not to be construed as real. Any resemblance to actual events or persons, living or dead, is entirely coincidental.

A CIP catalogue record for this book is available from the British Library.

ISBN 9781835406274 7777/3 JFMAMJJAS D/23

Printed and bound using 100% renewable electricity at CPI Group (UK) Ltd CR0 4YY.

MIX
Paper | Supporting responsible forestry
FSC www.fsc.org FSC® C171272

A Girl Called Corpse

REECE CARTER

ILLUSTRATIONS BY ELEONORA ASPARUHOVA

USBORNE

THE MANOR
ELSTON-FRIGHT
WRECKING HAZARD
Do not approach

ELSTON-FRIGHT
N
W
E
S
ANGLER ROCKS
THE CEMETERY
THE LIGHTHOUSE
Rock-That-Doesn't-Exist

Zero

If my hair looks like bright green seaweed, it's because that's exactly what it is. My eyes, a pair of abalone shells, polished blue by sand. Teeth, two rows of pebbles.

And my skin is made of wax.

I spent a very long time collecting the wax, I'll have you know, from *their* burning candles. And it was an extremely hard thing to do, too. I had to steal it, drip by drip, whenever *they* weren't watching. In the darkest parts of the night, I would whisk the wax away, little by little. And if one of them had ever bothered to glance up, they might very well have seen the glistening droplets that I was beckoning dance on the air, slip over rotting beams and disappear through a gap in the iron ceiling. But nobody ever looked up. Nobody noticed.

I made sure of that.

It took years to shape the wax into my sort-of-odd-looking head. My skinny neck and awkward shoulders. Arms and legs, which if I'm honest, are kind of knobbly.

Fine…so I'm not perfect looking.

But as skinny and awkward and knobbly as my wax body might be, it's still a million times better than having no body at all. That was the absolute worst. Maybe *some* ghosts enjoy walking through walls and being invisible – not me. I never wanted any of that.

I never asked to be a kid ghost.

I mean, I guess nobody really *asks* to be a ghost, do they? Nobody asks to wake up dead. Just like nobody asks to be snatched by Witches and taken from their families.

Wait…I didn't mention there are Witches, did I?

Well, there are.

But before you go and flip out, just remember that these particular Witches live far away from you, inside a rickety old shack built from rotting stilts and decaying scrap metal. A shack that is tucked deep inside the cave of an elephant-shaped rock.

And that rock is surrounded by sea.

If you were to ask most people – most *living* people, I mean – they would probably tell you that the rock I'm talking about doesn't even exist. I'm not saying that it's invisible, exactly. It's more like you forget that you've seen it the moment you stop looking at it. One minute it's there, clear as day. But as soon as your eyes slide past, it's like somebody has taken to your brain with a sponge. All that you remember is cold and empty ocean.

The rock-that-doesn't-exist sits off the coast from a town, nestled among trees, that nobody ever visits. Summer tourists don't register the little fishing village, or the empty lighthouse that looms over it, preferring instead the glitzy resorts and white-sand beaches up the way. Nobody stops to bother with the town, its people or its secrets. And even *I've* forgotten the town's name. But don't worry; I'm certain that it's nowhere near you.

Well...not *certain*, obviously.

I mean it has to be somewhere, doesn't it?

What I should say then is that it's *probably* nowhere near you – depending, I suppose, on exactly where it is that you are. But if you *do* happen to be somewhere near the town-that-nobody-visits, my advice would be to get out of there as quickly as you can. I'd tell you to grab your family and your friends and whatever else you care about, and run.

I'd tell you to keep running. Then run some more.

Because if where you are – where you are right this very second – is close to the town-that-nobody-visits, that would mean you're near the rock-that-doesn't-exist, too.

With its damp cave and its rickety shack. And its Witches.

Not that you'd know it, of course.

Chapter 1

I should probably introduce myself. I'm Corpse.

Obviously it's not the name I was born with. I forgot *that* one as soon as I died. If I've counted right, that means I forgot my name nearly thirteen years ago to the day. And if I had to guess, I'd say that's about the same number of years that I was alive, too.

Give or take.

I couldn't bring my name with me when I died, just like I couldn't bring any of my memories. When you become a ghost, every trace of your life vanishes. The faces of your family. The house where you lived. You even forget how it is that you died.

All of it just slips away, as if taken by the tides, and by the time your very last memory is gone, you can't help but wonder whether you might have just always been a ghost.

Every single memory from your life disappears...

...and all you're left with is questions.

That's why I call myself Corpse, I guess. Because I have no idea whether I was an Alice or an Annabelle. A Sophie or a Sarah. A Poppy or a Prudence.

Or anything else like that.

"What do you think of these?" I ask Simon now, holding a pair of periwinkles for him to see. I turn them this way and that, letting them catch the afternoon's silver light.

Click-click-click, he says.

"Hmm...maybe you're right."

I fling the periwinkles out to sea, where they disappear beneath the glassy surface. "But it's hard to find a pair that are *exactly* the same size, you know."

Click-click.

"I think you're being a bit fussy today, Simon."

Simon is a spider, by the way. A huntsman spider, to be exact.

He's got grey-brown fuzz, and eight wriggly legs that tickle my wax skin whenever he crawls across it. Right now, though, he's sitting on my shoulder.

"Come on then," I say. "Let's keep looking."

(Yes, I can talk to animals. All ghosts can.)

I hurry ahead, scampering over the tide pools that fringe the rock-that-doesn't-exist. And as I go, I scan underfoot for something that might work as a new set of ears. A pair of limpets, maybe? Matching ram's horns? A couple of dead jellyfish? Anything has got to be better than the sea squirts I've been using lately. They keep falling off. Every now and again I collect something, hold it up to the side of my head and ask Simon for his honest opinion. And every single time – *click-click-click-click!* – he suggests that we keep looking.

"Fine," I tell him. "But you're being *very* picky today."

I mean…it's not like I need ears, exactly. Not in the way that a fleshie does, anyway. Fleshies are what I call people who haven't died yet, and obviously *they* need ears.

(You know, to hear and stuff.)

Us ghosts, on the other hand, can hear perfectly fine without them. Just like how we can see without eyes and smell without noses. Still, I like having all those things.

Having them makes me feel less dead.

I guess it's lucky, then, that I discovered I'm different to other ghosts. I can do something that most others can't. In fact, there have been heaps of other kid ghosts who have come and gone from the rock-that-doesn't-exist, but I've never met any who were able to pour themselves into a body like I can. Not a single one. And being able to Possess this body…

…well, it's about as close to being alive as a ghost can be.

This body lets me touch stuff and remember what things feel like. I can pick things up. Move them around. But more important than any of that, having this body helps me stick around. It helps keep away the thing that comes *after* you turn into a ghost.

It helps keep me out of Death Proper's clutches.

"What about these?" I ask Simon now.

(This time, I'm holding a pair of violet snails.)

...*click*.

"No need to be rude," I grumble. "A simple 'no' would do."

And with a sigh, I toss the snails into the ocean.

Then, I hurry ahead.

I probably wouldn't admit it to him while he's being like this, but I'm glad that Simon comes on these beachcombing missions with me. Normally, spiders are very easily scared creatures, even though you wouldn't think it. They don't like to leave home much if they can help it. Not Simon, though. He's pretty brave for a spider.

"URGH!"

Shuddering, I pull my foot away from the soft and squishy something that I just stepped on. Even before I look down, I know what I'm going to find.

Yep...three dead cormorants.

Yuck.

The Witches did it. No doubt about that. I've seen

them do the spell a thousand times before. To leave the rock-that-doesn't-exist and cross the water to the town-that-nobody-visits, each of the three Witches first needs to steal the shape of a creature that can swim or fly. But this particular spell comes with a price, and today it's the cormorants who paid it.

"I really do *hate* the Witches," I say to Simon.

Click-click-click, he agrees.

I scan the skies, just in case, but there's nothing to see except steely and polished clouds. Further out to sea, the sky is beginning to grow inky and dangerous. The first signs of a coming storm dance on the air. But nope...there's no sign of the Witches.

(Still, I know they'll be back soon.)

"It's been hours since they left," I say.

Click-click.

"They've been away so much lately."

Click-click-click.

I only ever dare to step outside when the Witches are away from the rock-that-doesn't-exist because, somehow, they've never worked out that I haunt the roof above their shack. They have no clue that a ghost made of wax shares this place with them. And I can't *ever* let them find out that I do. I don't want to think about what would happen if they did.

Click-click-click, Simon says.

I nod. "Maybe a *little* bit longer."

Darting forwards, and accidentally startling a family of rock crabs as I go, I come to a stop beside a glassy pool, where I watch an octopus tuck himself into a crack. He's just finished disguising himself to look like a rock when I spot something pretty resting beside him.

"What about this?" I say.

I plunge my hand into the icy water and retrieve it. A chunk of amber sea glass. Running a thumb over it, I smile at how smooth and cool and hard it feels beneath my touch.

(Kind of like a jewel or something.)

"Yes, I *do* realize I would need two of them," I tell Simon, before he gets a chance to say something about needing more than one ear. "But it doesn't have to be an ear. Maybe it could be a nose! I haven't had a new nose in ages. What do you think?"

Click.

"Good," I say, and pocket the sea glass in my overalls. They're tatty and don't fit me properly, but I like them for my own reasons. "That's something, at least."

CLICK!

"What?"

CLICK-CLICK-CLICK!

Simon jabs one long and crooked leg back in the direction of the rock that houses the Witches' shack. In its shadow, an unfamiliar figure is shuffling towards us. Hunched over and slow, the figure is all invisible creases and blurred colours and shifting outlines. Another ghost, appeared as if from nowhere.

Only this ghost doesn't have a body. This ghost isn't like me. He's just a regular ghost. As he shuffles closer, a swooping gull passes right through him.

"Is that…is that an *old man ghost*?"

Hurrying to tuck myself behind a boulder sort-of-thing, I crouch down and peek around the side of it to get a better look. Only I still don't believe what I'm seeing.

"Why would an old man ghost be out here?"

Click-click? Simon suggests.

I shake my head. "No. The Witches didn't snatch him."

They only ever snatch kids, because when it comes to doing their most horrible magics and brewing their most disgusting concoctions, only kids are of any use to them.

He must have died at sea, then, or found some other way here.

Except that there *is* no other way here. No way on or off the rock-that-doesn't-exist. If there was, I would have found it by now. I've been looking for one since I got here.

"Wait…where is he?" I whisper.

I only looked away for a second, but now the old ghost is gone.

Something strange fizzes over my wax skin, dancing along the place where my spine should be, then wriggling up my neck. *Danger,* it seems to be warning me.

"Simon, did you see wh—"

"There you are."

The voice, grumbling and gruff, is coming from right behind me. I spin around to find that the old ghost isn't gone at all. My whole body turns rigid.

He takes a lumbering step forwards.

"Found you," he growls.

I jump up. "Go away."

All that fizzing energy rushes to my legs, making them feel like loaded springs. Every part of my body is tense and ready for action. Whoever this ghost is...

...he can't be good news.

Chapter 2

"Don't come any closer!" I warn him.

"Calm down, kid," the old ghost grumbles. "I'm a friend."

I feel myself frown.

A...*friend?*

Doubtful.

Up close he looks like a sack of potatoes. And he smells funny too – like wet wool and mouldy straw and stale tobacco. When he smiles, it's wide and crooked and mostly toothless. It's not a mean smile, or a scary one. It's not exactly friendly, either.

(I don't know what it is, but I *do* know that I don't trust it.)

"You *are* Corpse, aren't you?" he says.

I take another step away from him, tilt my head back and peer up at him. "Maybe. Depends on who's asking. Who are *you*?"

The old ghost shrugs. "Haven't got the foggiest, have I?"

I guess I should have expected that. Of course he doesn't remember who he is or what his name is because *no* ghost remembers who they are or what their name is. "Your friend calls me Old Man." He shrugs again. "Guess you can too…if you'd like."

There's that word again.

"I don't have any friends," I say automatically.

Click? Simon reminds me.

"Well yes," I whisper. "Obviously *you're* my friend."

The ghost who calls himself Old Man gives Simon a funny look but doesn't comment. I think maybe I see him smirk. "You have another friend too," he says to me. "And she asked me to bring you this message. Or…I suppose it's more of a warning, really." He turns around. Begins to shuffle away.

She?

"We don't have very long, though," he adds.

(But I don't follow him. No way.)

"Quickly now," Old Man says.

I don't take even a single step forwards. I just stand there. There's a familiar tickling sensation as Simon climbs his way up and into my hair. *Click-click?*

"Of course I'm not scared," I whisper back to him.

Click?

"I'm *not*."

And it's true. I'm not scared. Not really.

Fine. I guess I was a little bit surprised when Old Man appeared out of nowhere, but who wouldn't be? Anyway, being surprised and being scared are *not* the same thing.

It would be different if it was the Witches who found me out here. With a single spell, they could blast this wax body of mine to pieces, or else melt it into a big, sticky puddle. But Old Man is just another ghost. He can't hurt me. And so no, I'm not scared.

(Still...that doesn't mean I'm following him *anywhere*.)

"No," I call after him.

Old Man stops. Turns around.

"...No?"

"*No,*" I repeat, crossing my arms. "I'm not following you. I don't even know who you are! If some stranger turned up on your rock, would you follow them?"

Old Man frowns. "Not sure I have a rock."

"I'm not going anywhere until you tell me how you got here. Because I've haunted the rock-that-doesn't-exist for my entire death, I'll have you know." I uncross my arms just long enough to wave them around. "There's no way on or off it."

I expect him to argue...

...but instead, he chuckles.

"She didn't tell me you would be so stubborn," he says. And then he starts hobbling away in the other direction again, shaking his head as he goes. "Come on."

I still don't move. "*Who* didn't tell you?"

Then, I add, "What are you even talking about?"

He says over his shoulder, "Got a lot of big questions bouncing around that wax head of yours, don't you, kid? Questions that want answers."

Something wriggles where my stomach should be.

Answers?

Old Man keeps walking. "Well, if it's answers that you want, I might as well tell you that I know where to find 'em. But you'll need to follow me."

I can't help myself. I chase after him. "Wait up!"

I reach Old Man easily in just a few quick strides. He doesn't move very quickly. I keep up with him without even trying. "What *kind* of answers?"

I try to make it sound like I don't care.

(Even though I definitely do.)

"The type that matter," he replies simply.

Something warm flutters behind the place where my belly button should be. And at the same time, old and familiar questions push their way into my not-brain. They start multiplying, buzzing about like insects. Questions about my name. Questions about my family.

"How do you know about all that?" I ask.

"She told me."

"*Who* did?

"Your fr—"

Old Man stops in his tracks. He lifts a hand in front of his face as if to inspect it, and I notice with a strange jolt that it's beginning to turn more see-through.

Actually…

…*all* of him is beginning to turn more see-through.

As we stand there, Old Man grows more transparent. His edges become all smudged. I've seen this happen before, but it never gets easier to watch. This is what happens right before a ghost dies their second death. Right before they slip away into Death Proper.

"You're going…already?"

Old Man nods. "Got less time than I thought."

He leans closer, and when he speaks again his words come out all urgent-sounding. "Don't reckon I can put off second death very much longer," he says. "So, listen up, will you? Those Witches, they're up to something." A pause. "We need to get you off this rock."

I shake my head. "*Off* the rock-that-doesn't-exist? That's not even—"

"—possible?" he finishes for me.

And I nod.

"Course it is," he says. "I'll show you."

"I don't understand what any of this has to do with me."

According to Old Man, the reason that the Witches have been away from the rock-that-doesn't-exist so much lately is that they're hunting for some sort of treasure.

"What *kind* of treasure?" I ask as I follow him across the tide pools and rock flats.

"One that wasn't theirs to take in the first place," Old Man says, with something like a scowl. It's not exactly an answer. "Them Witches stole it years ago, then traded it with someone in that town." He points towards the town-that-nobody-visits. "Someone they call *the Merchant*."

"So…this Merchant person has the treasure?"

Old Man shakes his head. "The Merchant sold it. When the Witches went to take it back, the Merchant told 'em it was gone. Taken some place far away."

"Where is it now then?"

"Missing." He comes to a stop.

It's only now that I realize exactly where Old Man has brought me. We've come to a part of the rock-that-doesn't-exist that I *never* visit – not any more, anyway.

It's a place where the rock folds in on itself, carving out a jagged chasm sort-of-thing, with walls that soar overhead, casting the entire space in shadow. At high tide, rising waters form a pool along the bottom. Then when the waters rush back out, they leave behind big piles of sand and seaweed. Right now, the tide is growing higher and the water level rising.

Old Man steps down into the pool without making so much as a ripple. It's as if the bottoms of his legs vanish. What's left of him above the water is fading fast. The whole walk here, Death Proper's grip has been growing tighter on him. There's not much left now. Still, for a moment I think about just turning around and leaving him out here.

Because this place…I hate it.

This place reminds me of *her*.

"Come on," Old Man says. "Hurry up, kid."

I could easily outrun him. I could race back to my roof above the Witches' shack and seal it up tight. I could forget about this whole strange thing. But when

I glance back over my shoulder, I see the abandoned lighthouse in the distance. And beside it, the cemetery. From there, I gaze across the dark and huddled trees, towards the town with its fishing wharf and its winding roads and its little houses. The town-that-nobody-visits.

I must have lived there once, back before the Witches snatched me. I'm certain it's where my family must be waiting. Maybe they're even inside one of those little houses right this very moment.

Got a lot of big questions bouncing around that wax head of yours, don't you, kid?

Yeah, I do.

I turn back towards where Old Man is waiting for me, trying to forget the last time I was standing here.

And I step into the pool.

Water reaches all the way up to my knees, soaking my overalls. The cold stings against my wax skin. But I wade forwards anyway, following Old Man deeper into the water.

(And deeper into shadow too.)

He keeps squinting into each corner and muttering to himself. "Where is it?" he grumbles over and over. "She said it would be right here."

"What are we looking for?"

He points ahead of him. "That!"

All I can see is some shaggy mass piled up against the rock wall. It's a giant mound of seaweed – and to be honest it looks *exactly* like the ones either side of it.

"There's nothing there," I tell him.

"Wrong. Look closer."

A squirmy excitement springs to life when I realize that he's right. There *is* something there. A crescent of white like bones peeks from under the weed.

Without stopping to think, I dart forwards. I yank two armfuls of seaweed from the whatever-it-is. It breaks away in my grip, but I toss it to one side and hurry to grab more. Then more.

More and more.

Whatever it is that's buried beneath the seaweed, it's curved and made of timber that has begun to rot. It must have been here a while and turned soft with time. My wax fingers get peppered with little splinters as I work, but I don't stop until the thing is uncovered.

And once it is, I step back to take a better look.

It's a dinghy.

Barely big enough for two people, the boat must have washed up here during high tide and then become stuck.

"This is how you'll leave the rock and track down

that Merchant," Old Man says from behind me. "Then you can find the treasure and take it back."

That last part catches me off guard.

"What do you mean 'take it *back*'?"

I turn around to face Old Man just as he takes a step closer. For the first time since arriving on the rock-that-doesn't-exist, something like softness crosses his face.

Maybe even something like...*sadness*?

I finally realize what all this has to do with me.

"It's mine, isn't it?" I ask him. "The treasure is mine."

Old Man nods. "Told you earlier that the Witches *stole* this so-called treasure of theirs before they traded it with the Merchant. But what I didn't tell you is that the person they stole it from – the *kid* they stole it from – was someone they snatched."

He pauses. And the moment feels heavy.

"That someone was you," he finishes. "Find the thing the Witches call a treasure and you'll get back all those memories you're missing."

What kind of treasure can hold *actual* memories? I picture a crown that fills its wearer with wisdom, or maybe some golden conch shell that whispers secrets that sound like a sighing ocean.

"But what is it?" I ask him. "What *exactly*?"

Old Man still doesn't answer me. If anything, he looks like he wishes he'd never mentioned it at all. Or at the very least, like he didn't have to say this next part.

"What *is* it?" I repeat.

He sighs. "All right, kid."

And what he tells me next makes a chill pass up and over my wax skin. The cold seeps right through me. It reaches all the way to my not-chest, where it freezes over.

"They took...?" I begin.

Only, I can't say it. "They took...*that*?"

Old Man nods. "Twisted a theft as they come."

It feels like the air forgets that it's meant to be growing stormy. Everything turns still and silent. That's when I notice with a lurching feeling that Old Man has started to look like an ink drawing that somebody has spilled water all over. Right in front of me, his features are starting to lose their shape and bleed into one another. Simon must notice it too, because he chooses this moment to scuttle out from my hair, back to his place on my shoulder.

Click-click-click, he says to Old Man.

The old and fading ghost smirks again. Or maybe he just smiles. Maybe it's even kind. I can't tell. Either way, he says to Simon, "Take care of her, little spider."

Click-click, Simon promises.

"But…can't you come with me?" I ask.

Old Man shakes his head. "You know I can't do that. Already stayed longer than I should have." He pauses. "Just long enough to do one bit of good after a rotten life."

And then his eyes slip out of focus.

They turn all foggy and distant.

When he speaks again, his voice has become all staticky. Each word crackles and crunches. "Now there are two more things I need to say before I go. Firstly, I may not remember much from life, but there is one thing I know to be absolutely true, and that is that there's nothing more powerful or more terrifying than a kid acting with their whole heart."

I throw my hands up in the air. "That doesn't even make sense. *Stay*."

I know it's pointless, though. You can't stop second death.

Old Man's voice comes unstuck from the ghostly figure in front of me. It rustles all around me, like a breeze moving through tree leaves. "Secondly, the Witches have spread a sickness over that town. It's dangerous…but you won't be alone…she'll be…"

His voice fades to nothing before he can finish.

Silence floods in to take its place.

A few tiny crinkles mark the air, right at the place where he was standing only a few seconds ago. And as I watch, they lose their shape and vanish too.

Old Man is gone.

"Come back!" I shout – even though it's hopeless. I've seen enough ghosts slip away to know that they never come back. The old ghost who appeared on my rock as if from nowhere has vanished just as quickly now. And so, I don't really expect him to answer me. He does though. The sky swirls around me. Whispers one last word.

"*Go*," it seems to say.

CHAPTER 3

Even after I'm sure that Old Man has slipped into Death Proper for good, I don't drag the dinghy away from where it's wedged against the rock. I don't jump into it and glide out to sea. I don't head off in search of the thing he said the Witches stole from me.

Instead, with Simon in my hair, I turn and hurry away from that place.

I scamper back across the tide pools, then rush through the lightning-shaped entrance to the rock-that-doesn't-exist. I scale the cave wall, following the path I know well, and then leap onto the shack's roof. I drag aside a loose sheet of iron, and slip inside.

And then I just sit there, wrapped up in darkness.

My knees are tucked right under my chin.

My arms hug them tight.

Cre-e-e-ak. Cre-e-e-ak.

The growing winds can't touch me here, hidden inside the cave, but the shack sways and creaks anyway. From somewhere above there comes a steady and metallic dripping sound as drops of water fall from the cave roof, striking the corrugated iron.

Drip-drip-drip.

Drip-drip.

Drip.

"We're not going looking for it," I say eventually.

Click-click? Simon replies from overhead. Even though I can't see him, I know he's tucked away in the most cramped corner of the roof – his favourite spot.

"Because," I reply, "we're just not."

Click?

"Just...just *because*, Simon."

Because I should never have trusted some strange ghost who just showed up on my rock, I think. *Because it was silly to listen to Old Man, and maybe even dangerous to follow him. Because even if the treasure does exist – and I'm pretty sure that it doesn't – Old Man said that it's been sold now. That it was taken some place far away from here.*

And, well…I can't *go* far away, can I?

Not for long, anyway.

So even if I *did* believe Old Man – which I don't think that I do – and even if I *did* decide to take the dinghy – which I won't – I wouldn't be able to leave the rock-that-doesn't-exist for long. I'd have to come back here. Because I'm sort of stuck here. In a way.

I shake my head, trying to empty it of unwelcome thoughts.

Click-click-click?

"I don't know," I admit.

Truth is, no matter how much I rack my not-brain, I can't work out who Old Man might have been, or how he made it to the rock-that-doesn't-exist. He can't have come here in that old dinghy. Not without a body to work it. Besides, the dinghy has obviously been washed up here on the rock-that-doesn't-exist for months at least. Maybe years.

So then…how *did* he get here?

I don't have an answer. And if there's one thing I hate, it's questions without answers. I shake my head. Stand up. Dust myself off.

"No more questions," I tell Simon.

I decide that the very best thing I can do right now is to forget everything that Old Man told me. Pretending that something never happened is basically the same thing as it actually never happening, so I push today far from my not-brain and set to work doing totally normal things instead. I walk over to the gap in the roof I just crawled through, and I drag the sheet of iron back across it. Then, I say the words that will secure it in place.

(The words that will keep us safe from prying eyes.)

"Moss on stone and flesh on bone," I begin, drawing my hands through the air and reciting the words that I know by heart. "Wings on bat and tail on cat."

It's probably worth pointing out that when you've haunted a Witches' shack for as long as I have, you can't help but pick up a few of their tricks. It took me ages to learn them, and even longer to get them just right, but now I know three simple magics of my own.

A fire hex, a beckoning charm…

…and this sticking spell.

"Like the beak is on a duck," I say, as magic starts to hum in the air all around me. It makes the dust puff and swirl. "Make these two things good and stuck."

A loud *SQUELCH!* tells me that the spell worked.

"There," I say, satisfied. "Good."

Cre-e-e-ak. Cre-e-e-ak.

Drip-drip-drip.

The roof sighs and groans around me, and it reminds me how this shack never used to be a shack at all. Back when I first woke up here as a ghost, it was a house, sturdy and strong. But then after a while the walls started bending. The beams started buckling. And even though the Witches patch it up with sticking spells, they never last long.

It's like the shack *wants* to fall apart or something.

I try to ignore it, and step towards the upside-down wooden crate sitting in the very centre of the floor. Like the rest of this place, it's coated in a thick layer of grime. And sitting on top of it is a tallow candle – short, and half burned already. "Flint and spark will light the dark," I begin, wriggling my wax fingers as I go. Magic begins to dance.

"Birch and fern, they both must burn."

I imagine my pointing finger to have a tiny flame flickering at its end. "For Witches died on the pyre," I say. "Grant me this one wish for fire."

Snap. Crack. Fizzle.

My fingertip ignites like a match.

I touch the wick of the candle and my roof comes alive with a warm and flickering glow. It throws shadows all around me – unwelcome shadows that twist and bend themselves into the familiar figures of ghosts who have come and gone from this place. Ghosts who have already slipped into Death Proper. Ghosts whose real names I never knew.

The Crying One. The Two Twins. The Silent Kid. And up in the rafters, dancing and twirling like she used to do, is a shadow that looks just like Girl.

Girl.

Simon never met her, but she was the last ghost to haunt this roof with me. Girl stayed longer than any

other ghost, and I don't know how she did it. Usually, a ghost only sticks around long enough to accept that they're dead. Then, once they're used to the fact their life is over, Death Proper takes them. My wax body keeps me safe from Death Proper, but Girl didn't have one of those. Somehow, though, she managed to stay. For two whole years.

I guess you could even say she became my friend.

Together, Girl and I were going to find a way off the rock-that-doesn't-exist. We were going to head for the town-that-nobody-visits to track down our families. We would find out who we were and learn our names. But then one day, nearly a year ago –

No. I don't want to think about that day.

"Go away," I say to the shadows.

Pushing Girl from my not-brain, I turn my attention

instead to the battered enamel bowl that sits beside the candle, and that is filled with the trinkets I've found during my beachcombing adventures across the tide pools. Shiny fishing lures. Bright plastic baubles. There's even a couple of dried-up starfish. I pluck the amber sea glass from earlier out of my pocket and place it on top of the pile, then collect up my favourite belonging of all.

A single black button – plain in every way.

Except that it *isn't* plain.

Not to me.

I turn the button over in my hand. Run a thumb across it. And as I do, the shadow illusions twist into the shape of the family I never met. It makes something in my not-chest ache. When I tuck the button in my pocket, the pain eases. The icy feeling that I haven't been able to shake since Old Man told me about the Witches' treasure thaws just a little bit.

Down below, the front door slams. The whole shack shakes.

I hurry to smother the tallow candle.

"Simon," I hiss. "They're back."

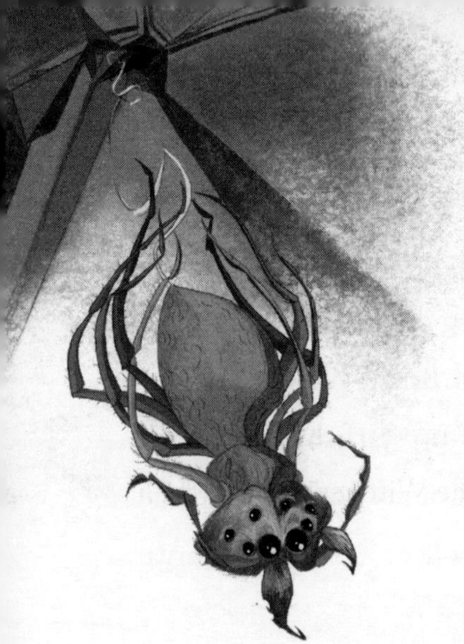

Click-click-click.

I point my open hands in the direction of his corner. "Out of luck and out of reach," I mutter, calling magic to me. "You I need, you I beseech." I picture Simon flying towards me. "Thing I seek, please come hither," I say. Then lastly, "Hurry now, don't you dither."

There's a *ping!* when Simon is shot from his corner. And a *whoosh!* as he zips into my hands.

I place him on my shoulder, then carefully drop to my knees without making a sound. My fingers trace through the grime. They move over ridges and grooves until I find the little gap in the ceiling that gives me a view of the room below. I press one abalone shell eye up close to it, but it's as dark down in the shack as it is up here. I can't see a single thing.

At least, not until somebody down there does a spell.

Fizzle. Snap. Crack. Snap. Fizzle.

The hundred candles that line the walls of the shack all light up at once, revealing the room beneath me. Every part of it is familiar. From here I can see the fire pit in its centre, and the tall book stand that holds the spell book *Magikal Maledictions*. Directly below me is the concoction bench where the Witches prepare their various potions and poultices.

And then there are the three Witches themselves.

Chapter 4

Most people think Witches are crooked old ladies, but that's not right at all. Anyone can be a Witch. As it happens, all the Witches *I've* ever known have been men.

Cruel and wicked men.

"That ssslipppery, ssslithering thief," curses the first of them. He paces around the fire pit below, his hands clenching and unclenching. "That duplicitousss sssnake."

Gorflunk the Witch has sparkling amethyst eyes from a spell gone right, and an eel's tail where his tongue should be from a spell gone wrong. Like always, he's wearing head-to-toe seal fur, sleek and shiny. Midnight hair cascades down and over his shoulders.

A second Witch barges past him, shuffling towards the book stand.

"Leave this to Scraggleknee," he says.

Scraggleknee *always* talks about himself like that – as if he's speaking about someone else entirely. Carbuncled, short and with lips that curve downwards like a stonefish, he wears layered robes the colour of a churned-up seabed. Only his barnacled hands, poking out from his sleeves and tipped with long and yellowed fingernails, give away that he isn't just some walking pile of rags. He starts flicking through the pages of *Magikal Maledictions*.

"But which spell?" he mutters. "Which spell for our revenge?"

A third voice sounds out from by the door.

"Inspiring as I find your hunger for vengeance, Scraggleknee," says the final Witch, in a voice that is cold and raspy and dry, "we have more pressing concerns." He crosses the floor in long and hurried strides, coming to a stop at the concoction bench.

Eyes, glowing like embers, sweep up towards me.

I dart back into shadow.

Scrambling away from the crack in the ceiling, my whole body starts to shiver. Seconds stretch out...but no flash of magic brings my roof crashing down.

I'm not blasted to pieces or melted into a puddle.

Before I can stop him, Simon jumps down from my shoulder and scurries back to the crack of light. He perches right at its edge and peers through it, checking to see what's going on down below. After a moment, Simon tells me the coast is clear.

(*Click-click-click!*)

Something inside me unclenches.

Slowly – and *very* carefully – I edge back towards the gap in the ceiling. When I glance through it, the Witch with the glowing ember eyes and deep sockets has looked away already. From here, though, I can hear his every rattling breath. Pale, tall and ancient, the third Witch reminds me of a teetering tower of ash. I don't actually know his name, because the others only ever address him as *Master* or *Sir*, so I've always just called him Worst-Witch.

"The rock is almost dead," he wheezes. "Even now I feel the Spellspring's magic fading from its very bones. It is only a matter of days before we run out completely."

Something deep in my not-belly churns.

A dying rock? A fading Spellspring?

Worst…a matter of *days*?

Click? Simon asks.

"The rock-that-doesn't-exist isn't a normal rock," I explain, whispering even though I really don't have to. It's not like the Witches can hear me or anything. Because the Witches are fleshies – and unlike animals, fleshies can't hear the voices of the dead.

I tell Simon that the rock-that-doesn't-exist is a Spellspring – a well of magic. I tell him there is a seam of sparkling ore that runs deep beneath the rock, and that the Witches draw magic from it, charging themselves with the stuff so that they can turn it into their spells later. I tell him that without the Spellspring, the Witches would have no magic at all.

But what I *don't* tell him is that they're not the only ones.

I don't know why I've never told Simon where my magic comes from. He's always just thought I was a kid ghost who could do spells, and I let him keep thinking it. But that's not right. Nobody can just *do* spells. That's not how it works. Everyone has to get their magic from somewhere, and I get mine from the same Spellspring as the Witches. Maybe *that's* why I never told him then. Maybe I didn't want him knowing that I'm like the Witches.

(In that one small and very unimportant way, at least.)

Or maybe it's that I didn't want him to know that I'm stuck on this rock. That if I left it, I'd run out of magic in no time. And that without my magic, I wouldn't be able to use my sticking spell to put my abalone shell eyes back on whenever they fall off or glue my seaweed hair back in place when it comes unstuck. I wouldn't be able to use my fire hex to melt and reshape the wax that I'm made from. And that if my whole body fell apart, and my ghostly self slipped back out of it, that Death Proper might be waiting to take me. Yeah, maybe that's it. Maybe I didn't want to admit to Simon that I was...well, not *scared*, exactly.

But something kind of like it.

Click-click-click? Simon asks me now.

I nod. "The Witches must have drained it dry."

(I didn't even know that could *happen* to Spellsprings.)

Down below us, Worst-Witch pulls a creased and yellowing paper from his pocket. Inspects it. "As usual, my instincts were correct," he wheezes. "The treacherous Merchant never sold our treasure at all. It has been here this whole time...right under our noses."

I feel my seaweed hair begin to prickle.

"Did he say their *treasure*?"

Click-click!

"The one Old Man told us about?"

Click!

"It's...*real?*"

"We were fools to let it out of our clutches," Scraggleknee spits from down below. "When we took it from the child years ago. We should have known—"

Worst-Witch holds up a hand to silence him.

"Cease your pointless yabbering."

Worst-Witch drops the paper on the concoction bench, and then opens it to reveal a map. I can see the wharf and the lighthouse and the bays marked on it. The hills and the surrounding forest are there too, as well as a meandering creek that runs through them. The only thing that's missing from the map is the rock-that-doesn't-exist. Obviously.

"But why do they even want it?" I whisper to Simon.

That's the part that doesn't make sense. Because the thing they took from me – *if* it really is what Old Man said that it is – is full of *my* memories. Not theirs.

So then…why do they want it so badly?

I strain to get a better look at the map over Worst-Witch's shoulder.

Someone has written on it in red ink. The entire thing is marked with circles and lines and arrows. The word *WITCHES* is scrawled across it over and over and over, at first in handwriting that is curly and neat, but which then turns messy and desperate.

WITCHES. WITCHES. WITCHES. WITCHES.

"Since the treasure was not at the Merchant's home," Worst-Witch wheezes, tracing a finger over the map, "it follows that it must be hidden in her Ungeneral Store."

He stands up tall. Folds the map.

And then he pockets it.

Worst-Witch starts opening and closing the drawers of the concoction bench, searching for something. His fingers move quickly – urgently, even – until he finds a small vial of something green. Whatever it is, it glows faintly. And when he unstoppers it…

…a stink like dead blowfish wafts up to my roof.

I pull away. "YUCK!"

But Worst-Witch is already pouring a little of the concoction into his mouth. As soon as it touches his tongue, something gross ripples beneath the Witch's papery skin.

"A deduction decoction," says Scraggleknee, approvingly.

Worst-Witch nods. "To sharpen our wits for the hunt."

"Geniusss, asss alwaysss, Sssir," Gorflunk says.

Worst-Witch passes the vial to Scraggleknee, who snatches it up. He takes a sip, and then his skin wriggles too – like there are maggots crawling beneath it – but it barely lasts a second. Gorflunk reaches and takes the vial from Scraggleknee.

He finishes the rest of it in one gulp.

Worst-Witch is holding a second vial now, this one filled with a black and swirling smoke that glitters faintly. "And a veiling tonic," he says, "to wrap the night around us."

Gorflunk leers. "For the element of sssurprissse."

This time, the Witches take turns inhaling from the vial. The smoke twists itself into threads that disappear right up their nostrils. And at the same time, it's almost like the candlelight decides to shy away from them. The air around the Witches turns darker.

Shadows collect at their edges.

"And most importantly," Worst-Witch rasps next, turning back towards the drawers and riffling through them. "Malicewater. To stretch our fading powers."

But he doesn't find it in the first drawer.

Or the second. Or even the third.

"Where is the malicewater?" he mutters.

Once Worst-Witch has checked every single drawer

along the concoction bench twice and still not found what he's looking for, he spins around. Glares at the others.

"*Who* drank the last of the malicewater?" he snarls at them.

Gorflunk shuffles on the spot. "Sssir—"

Worst-Witch's eyes glow red.

He looms over Gorflunk.

"Forgive me, Sssir," murmurs Gorflunk. "With the Ssspellssspring fading, my ssspellsss have been weak. I needed the malicewater, you underssstand. But I can make more."

Worst-Witch holds up a hand to silence him.

"Understanding is *not* in my nature," he sneers.

Worst-Witch raises his other hand. Magic begins to collect at his fingertips. I can see it from my roof. The air quivers for him, just like it does for me. I cup a hand over Simon so that he won't have to see whatever ugly magic Worst-Witch is about to unleash on Gorflunk as punishment.

Only nothing happens. Nothing at all. Worst-Witch's spell sputters out.

And the magic dissolves.

Gorflunk sighs with relief, but Scraggleknee seems disappointed. And if anything, Worst-Witch looks even angrier than he did before.

I let Simon out from under my hand.

"Their magic really *is* fading," I say.

Simon scuttles over my fingers and up my arm, taking his place on my shoulder. Down below, Worst-Witch stands at his fullest height over Gorflunk. "Do I need to remind you, Gorflunk, that every second wasted is another second magic leaves this place?"

"Then why delay?" interrupts Scraggleknee with a growl. "Scraggleknee has waited a long time for this moment." He steps closer. "Let us kill the Merchant *now.*"

Worst-Witch rounds on him.

"And you would have us do that *without* malicewater, would you?" Worst-Witch says. He glances from Scraggleknee to Gorflunk and then back again, and his face twists into a scowl. "The two of you are as useless as each other. Have you forgotten that until the treasure reunites us with magic, we rely *entirely* on our concoctions to sustain us?"

The fluttering from earlier returns.

"Did you hear that, Simon?"

"You have one hour," Worst-Witch says to the other two Witches, turning on his heel and marching towards the next room. "Prepare the malicewater exactly as prescribed in *Magikal Maledictions*." He pauses. Turns back. "And then hide the book."

Gorflunk bows. "Yesss, Sssir. Of courssse, Sssir."

"Leave it to Scraggleknee, Master," says Scraggleknee.

"Hide the book *well*," Worst-Witch repeats.

Then he leaves.

I sit up.

Down below, Gorflunk and Scraggleknee scramble to make a fresh batch of their malicewater, but Worst-Witch's words ring so loudly at the place where my ears should be that I can't hear anything they're saying. *Until the treasure reunites us with magic.*

And suddenly I know why they want it so badly.

The back of my neck begins to tingle, pushing aside the icy feeling I've been trying to shake ever since Old Man left. "Simon," I hiss. "We have to go."

Click?

I jump up, and without making a sound I hurry over to the loose sheet of iron in the roof. To do the un-spell and make it came unstuck, all I have to do is think of the magic words, and then twist them back to front. "Kcuts dna doog sgniht owt eseht ekam. Kcud a no si kaeb eht ekil. Tac no liat dna tab no sgniw," I say. "Enob no hself dna enots no ssom."

There's a *slurping* sound when it comes unstuck.

I drag the sheet of iron aside.

Click? Simon asks again.

"You know where," I reply.

Simon springs up happily. He scampers down my arm to my hand, where he begins to jump up and down in my palm. He scurries between my fingers. Runs in a circle.

Click-click-click!

"I'll explain on the way."

The tingling at the back of my neck has moved over my shoulders and across my arms. Now it's streaming down my back and all the way to my toes. Soon, every part of me is fizzing with something I can't name.

"We only have an hour," I say to Simon. "The Witches won't be far behind us."

Then, despite everything, a smile creeps across my face.

"And *we* have a treasure to find before they do," I say.

Chapter 5

On my way out of the cave, I creep slowly. I keep to the shadows in case any of the Witches happen to look out of the window. But by the time I hit the tide pools, I'm running.

The soles of my feet *thump* against the rock flats, my seaweed hair shakes and the electric something from before tingles all over my body. I hurry towards the place where the dinghy is waiting for us, explaining everything to Simon as I go, like I promised I would. I tell him how, like the Witches, I take my magic from deep beneath the rock-that-doesn't-exist. I tell him how, now that the Spellspring's magic is running out, we can't stay here.

And then I tell him how none of that matters anyway.

"Because there's a *second* Spellspring," I say.

Click-click? he asks.

I shake my head.

"I don't know what it is."

Another rock out to sea, maybe? Or perhaps one of the hills that surround the town-that-nobody-visits? A sea cave, even? I have no idea what it might be.

"But I *do* know the treasure will take us there."

Click?

"*How* do I know? Because Worst-Witch said the treasure would reunite them with magic. And that *has* to mean that somewhere inside it – somewhere with all of my other memories – there must be one that will tell them where the other Spellspring is."

...*Click-click?*

"It's the only explanation," I tell Simon.

Click-click-click?

I frown. "I don't know what that map was."

It doesn't take us long to reach the place where the rock-that-doesn't-exist folds in on itself. The place where Old Man vanished from and moved on. Only…

…the tide has risen now. The pool is *way* deeper.

It makes me pause.

Because ghosts can't swim.

(Come to think of it, I'm pretty sure spiders can't either.)

I glance over my shoulder, back the way I came. Then, I look out over the town-that-nobody-visits. Little yellow squares are starting to appear against the white houses. Families lighting their homes for the night. Loved ones gathering together, protected from the coming storm. *Which one is mine?* I wonder. *And who will be waiting for me inside?*

I tap at the pocket of my overalls.

The little black button is there.

Good.

I lower myself carefully into the water. It comes all the way up to my waist now, and if anything burns even colder than earlier. Wading through it has become harder, too.

Overhead, the sky is turning dark. Mean clouds

gather in the distance. They churn and swirl there, dropping a sheet of grey into the waiting sea below. We need to move quickly if we're going to cross the water before the storm arrives. We have to hurry.

"We need to get there before the Witches do," I say to Simon.

Click-click-click? he replies from my shoulder.

"To the Ungeneral Store," I tell him.

(Wherever that is.)

I grab the dinghy and pull it away from where it's wedged against the rock. It lands right way up with a *SPLASH!* It glides away, then spins around on the spot.

(Like it's waiting for me.)

I wade after it. Underneath the water, ugly brown wrasse with long stripes peck curiously at my nubby toes – like maybe they're food. I kick them away.

"Stop it," I tell them. "Those are mine."

They wriggle away looking offended, but I don't have time to worry about the feelings of fish right now. I collect Simon in my hand and place him on the boat's edge.

"In you get," I tell him.

...*Click?*

I smile at him. "You'll be okay. Find somewhere dry to hide."

Simon scurries off, and with a grunt I heave myself over the side after him. I topple into the boat, landing with a *thud*. Straight away, I'm struck by the smell of rot and stink and engine oil. The hull is even softer than I thought. The timber bends under my weight. I scramble to find a sturdier seat, and then peer around. There's nothing at all where the motor should be, but there are two old and battered oars on the floor. I collect them and, after a few minutes spent working out which end goes where, manage to get them into the mechanism things.

And when I drop the paddle ends into the water –

They make a satisfying *SPLASH!*

I grab the oars and we glide across the pool, out into the open waters. Once we're a little way off the rock-that-doesn't-exist, I stop and turn back to look at it.

Because I can't help myself.

This is the furthest I've been from the rock – in death, at least.

Looking back, it's hard to believe I didn't notice how much the rock-that-doesn't-exist has changed. When I woke up as a ghost, the rock was rusty red and decorated with splashes of turquoise lichen. Now, the whole thing is dull and grey. Like Worst-Witch's failed spell and the crumbling shack, it's just another sign of the magic being drained from this place.

How long will my magic last away from it? I wonder.

The thought makes me shiver.

It was different back when Girl and I were planning to leave the rock together. Don't ask me why. I just knew that when I was with her, everything would be all right. I knew that if we *did* find a way to the town-that-nobody-visits, Girl wouldn't let anything bad happen to me. But Girl is gone now. Like the others, she slipped away to Death Proper.

In the distance, thunder rumbles.

"We should get moving," I say.

We need to hurry if we're going to get to the Ungeneral Store before the Witches. We need to hurry if we're going to find the so-called treasure that is waiting for us there. The one that will remind me of my name and take me back to my family. The one that will lead me to the second Spellspring, so that I can keep on doing my magic for ever, free from the Witches. In other words, the treasure that will give me everything I've wanted for my entire death.

My whole body starts to tingle again.

It's like the ocean air comes alive around me.

I glance again at the town-that-nobody-visits. At the place where my answers are waiting. Then, I take one last look at the rock-that-doesn't-exist.

And I heave on the oars.

We're past the reef and over sand. The water is deeper here, and the distance between us and the shore is shrinking. The crescent-shaped beach is growing wider. Behind us, the storm is rolling closer and closer. The wind picks up.

A suddenly seasick Simon clicks sadly.

"We're nearly there," I lie.

(He doesn't reply.)

Just then, we hit a patch of kelp. Wide and flat

ribbons of the stuff, furling and unfurling in the currents, swarming around the dinghy. I row harder to get past it…

…but the boat slows right down.

The oars catch on the thick mass.

With a grunt, I –

"Wait. What was that?"

I let go of the oars. Lean over the edge. There's nothing to see except heaps of kelp. Still, for a second I could have sworn that I saw –

"There!"

A gleam of silver.

I try to get a closer look, but whatever it is simply vanishes into the folds again. All that's left is slippery, slimy kelp, dancing just beneath the surface.

"Simon?"

He crawls out from his hiding place, wobbly and lopsided. He staggers up and over my arm, back to his perch on my shoulder. A shiver follows close behind.

Click?

"It's nothing," I tell him, trying and failing to shake the uneasy feeling that it *wasn't* nothing. "I just wanted to check you were okay."

He clicks again. I straighten back up and tell myself that I'm seeing things. That kelp is only kelp. I keep paddling, until pretty soon, we're back over sand.

Then, over kelp again. It churns the water around us.

Ripples. Swells. Sloshes.

If I didn't know better – which I do – I'd say the kelp was moving in the opposite direction of the ocean and its currents. But that can't be right. Kelp can't move. Not like a fish can, anyway. Kelp can't make waters surge and heave...can it?

THUNK!

Something bumps against the bottom of the boat. Something *big*. Another tingle crosses my wax skin – this time from the top of my head, over the back of my neck and down my would-be spine. "Hold on," I warn Simon, and I paddle harder. But no sooner are we over clear waters than the kelp is under us again. Like it's *following* us.

THUNK! THUNK!

"Go away!" I shout. "We're not scared of you!"

THUNK! THUNK! THUNK!

This time, the whole boat rocks violently. Water sloshes up and over the side. The sea grows more agitated. It turns choppy and foamy and rough. The kelp has grown so dense now that it blocks out everything that lies beneath it. Except…there!

Another flash of silver.

"Simon!" I hiss. "Did you see—"

CLICK-CLICK-CLICK!

I don't need to be told twice. I dig the oars deep into the water and heave with every bit of strength I've got. But the oars just get all tangled up. And then –

Something heaves back.

SPLASH! One of the oars is ripped from my hand.

I fall backwards. Scramble to peer over the edge. The oar is all wrapped in kelp. Kelp that – there's no denying it now – is contracting like a python around its prey.

SNAP!

The oar is broken in two and the pieces dragged underwater. At the same moment, a big silver eye opens. Round like a dinner plate. Shiny. Flat.

Its pupil narrows when it sees me.

It blinks once. Twice.

CLICK-CLICK!

Without thinking, I grab the second oar.

CLICK-CLICK-CLICK!

I tell Simon to shush, then plunge the pointiest bit right into the kelpy thing's open eye. It vanishes beneath a slimy eyelid as a horrible and screeching cry sounds from somewhere just beneath the boat. The sound sends shockwaves across the surface.

I raise the oar over my head. "Leave us alone!"

But the ocean keeps growing angrier. It growls and it churns. Water is already up to my ankles, and the boat rocks wildly with every movement that I make.

The eye opens again, bloodshot now.

I stab again.

More screeching.

And again.

This time, the monster retreats. Sinks deeper. A few seconds later, there's nothing beneath us at all except the sandy ocean floor. It's like the thing just…

…dissolved.

A moment passes. Nothing happens.

The swell starts to calm.

"I…I think it's gone?" I tell Simon eventually, collecting him from my shoulder and bringing him up to my eye. "See? No need to be scared. Not when I've got you."

That's when the dinghy explodes.

Chapter 6

A sand-coloured tentacle shoots up from the deep and smashes through the hull.

All around us, an eruption of splinters.

"Wo-ARGH!" I cry.

The thing that is definitely *not* kelp loops itself around the little wooden dinghy and squeezes. The timber strains. It bends and buckles and crunches.

Cr-e-e-e-a-a-k.

Cr-e-e-e-e-e-a-a-a-k.

I wrap Simon up in my hand and press him close to my not-chest as what's left of the boat is dragged under water – with us in it. Ice-cold water burns against my wax skin. The monster's tentacles whip everything into a frenzy. Whorls of chaotic bubbles flood my vision, obscuring the surface. Simon and I are thrown back and forth and up and down, while chunks of our boat sink to the depths. I grab at the water. Try kicking to the surface.

But the drag is too strong.

It's not that I'm scared of drowning or anything. I don't need to breathe, after all. But Simon does. And so, I have to get him out of here. I have to get *us* out of here.

Only – I have a tentacle wrapped around me now.

I try to drag myself free, but struggling against it does nothing. The monster only grips me tighter when I do. I wish I could just leave this body. Slip out of it and escape.

Except I can't do that.

Leaving my body would mean leaving myself wide open to slip away into Death Proper. There is one other way. Another way I could get out of this…

…only I promised I would *never* do that ever again.

(And besides, Simon needs me.)

"Flint and spark will light the dark," I start instead, and I'm surprised to hear my words cut through the water as easily as if we were still above the surface. Hopefully, my magic will work down here too. "Birch and fern, they both must burn," I say, holding my free hand out in front of me. "For Witches died on the pyre. Grant me this one wish for fire."

Searing heat. Wriggling water. Steam-filled spheres.

I'm not sure how I expected my fire hex to turn out underwater – waterproof flames, maybe? – but what actually happens is that my hand begins to simmer and bubble like the bottom of a cauldron. I reach out and press it against –

"SKWEEE-oargh!"

The monster screeches. It recoils, and I slip free. I kick away from it. And as I do, I notice a raw and fleshy handprint has sprung to life on its tentacle, right where I touched it. The monster grabs at me again. Catches me around the neck. I press my bubbling hand against it – *SKWEEE-oargh!* – and it releases me again. I expect to keep sinking.

But I don't.

(I guess wax floats?)

Looking down beneath me, I see the mass of slimy tentacles flash green. They turn back to the colour of sand, but only for a second. Then, they go green again.

Now purple. So dark they're almost black.

Green. White. Orange.

Purple again. The monster retreats to the ocean floor.

I'm *just* about to break the surface – "Hold on, Simon" – when I notice all sixteen of the monster's tentacles straighten out beneath its big and balloon-shaped body.

It's preparing to attack me again.

Then, two silver eyes appear. They narrow in on me. Its tentacles contract like springs.

Panic snuffs out my magic.

I kick harder.

But the monster has already shot up and grabbed me by the ankle. I start to summon fire again when I realize that the monster isn't dragging me downwards at all. Instead, it's actually pushing me *upwards*.

I explode back out of the water. Come to a stop.

I'm hanging upside down above the waves.

"Simon! Are you okay?"

He's scrunched up in a tiny little ball, right in the very centre of my palm, with his legs folded up and over his body. He doesn't move. He doesn't even *click*.

"Please be okay," I whisper.

Something does a backflip in the place where my tummy should be when the tentacle holding me begins to circle like a lasso. Slowly, at first. Then faster. And faster still.

"PUT ME DOWN!" I shout.

I clamp my hand shut again to keep Simon safe as we whirl and twirl, spinning around faster and faster. My body flops about. It flails this way and that. Tangled seaweed hair covers my face, and I can't see a thing. "Let us go!" I yell. "LET US—wo-ARGH!"

I soar high over the ocean, faster than I've ever moved before. Possibly faster than I've seen *anything* move before. Air whips my skin and the smell of salt floods my senses. I worry that I'm going to crash back into the water, but it never happens. Instead, I just keep rocketing ahead, straight towards the half-moon stretch of beach. I keep going and going…

…the beach grows closer…

…until I land on the sand with a *THUD!*

My limbs crumple under my weight. My face slams hard into the ground. I roll forwards once. Twice. Then

I come to a stop and sit up. But when I open my hand again, Simon is still completely motionless. "Simon!" I say. "Simon, please wake up…"

A leg quivers. Flicks. Stretches.

One by one, the rest do the same.

I hold him close to me and listen for a…

…

…

…*click.*

For a second, I wonder whether I even heard it at all. It's so soft – more like a scratching sound than anything else. But yes, it's definitely there. Without knowing where it comes from, I pull him to my not-chest and wrap him up in a hug. "Simon, you're okay!"

Click…click…

"I'm just glad that you—"

CLICK!

"Oh," I say, relaxing my grip. "Right. Sorry."

(Got to be careful not to squish him.)

SLUUURP-WOOSH!

The sound comes from near the shoreline.

Even before I look up, I know the monster has arrived.

Sure enough, its bulbous head and silver coin eyes poke above the surface. Its tentacles tickle the water around it. One reaches forwards, out of the water. A second follows.

A third and a fourth. The monster drags itself up onto the sand.

Then a fifth and sixth tentacle emerge.

The monster moves closer, past the line where the sea meets the sand, towards where Simon and I are sitting. I should get up. I should run.

But I can't.

The monster lifts itself to its full and towering height, teetering on sixteen tentacles that look like stilts. Shakily, uncertainly, it starts walking in our direction.

That's when it starts to change.

Its kelp-like tentacles fold and braid and knot. They weave themselves together and pull tight. Simon wobbles up my arm, over my shoulder, and hides in my seaweed hair.

When the thing comes to a stop, transformation complete –

The monster has become a *person*.

An impossibly tall person, that is, made entirely of woven kelp.

Their eyes are silver and flat, like those belonging to a fish. Spines like blades extend from the place where their fingers should be. Gills flare, fleshy and gross.

Quickly, I do my fire hex again.

But nothing happens. My fingertips just smoke and steam and sizzle a whole heap. The monster snarls, stumbling back. They tilt their head from side to side and squint.

(Almost as if trying to get a better look at me.)

"Why did you let us go?" I demand.

Then, "Wait…*did* you let us go?"

Something isn't right. The monster could take me out in an instant if they wanted to, but they don't. Instead, they lean forwards slowly, reaching out in front of them with one long spine, and start writing something in the sand. They gesture for me to come closer.

In the fading light, I can just make out what's written:

GOST OR WEETCH?

"Huh? Gost or…*weetch*?"

They nod.

(I guess monsters, like animals, can understand ghosts.)

"Oh!" I realize suddenly. "You mean GHOST OR WITCH!"

The monster nods again.

"I'm a ghost."

Thinking on it, I add, "I mean…I suppose I'm *kind* of a Witch, because I know spells." But then I catch the look on their face. "No! No! I'm a ghost, don't worry."

The monster beams, teeth like needles.

They press their hands together and jerk their head up and down in a way that almost looks like a bow. Or even an apology.

But why would a spiny sea monster *apologize* to me?

Something tickles against the side of my neck. It's Simon, come to see what's going on. The monster leans down again. This time, they write:

YOO R KORPSE?

"Yes," I say cautiously. "I'm Corpse."

The sea monster starts bowing again, this time more vigorously. They point over my shoulder, beyond the trees behind me and towards the town-that-nobody-visits.

"That's where I'm going," I tell them.

And when they lean down again:

BEE CAERFULL

I nod.

But this is *very* strange.

NEED HALP? they write in the sand.

(They jab a spindly finger in my direction, then at themself.)

Then…

FYND WATTER

(They point out over the ocean.)

Then, with one last bow, the monster turns and stumbles back to the sea. And as they collapse into the water, I watch their body unknot until they look once more like the giant, wriggly kelp octopus that attacked us. Silver eyes flash in my direction.

The monster disappears.

CHAPTER 7

I guess the town-that-nobody-visits has a name after all.

The sign that marks the town's border is battered and broken. The pigment in its peeling paint has faded to bone white. Hanging from two rusty hooks, the sign *sque-e-e-e-aks* as it swings in the breeze – a breeze that is beginning to muster strength.

The storm is getting closer.

Click-click-click, says Simon.

He's made a complete recovery now, and has taken up his place perched on my shoulder again. But he just *won't* be quiet. *Click-click-click-click-click*, he pushes.

And when I don't answer him…

…*click-click?*

"I don't know," I say, for what must be the hundredth time, doing my best not to sound annoyed, even though I am. I do realize that Simon almost drowned just now, but I *really* hate questions I don't have answers for, and he knows it. So then *why* does he keep asking? I shake my head. "I have no idea why that monster let us go, all right?"

Click?

"No…I don't know how they knew my name, either."

Quietly, I agree with Simon that the whole thing was *highly* unusual. It's just that right now we've got something important to do. There's no time to get distracted.

Click-click –

"Enough questions," I interrupt. "The Witches will be here soon, and we have to find the Ungeneral Store before they get there. Can we *please* focus on that?"

...click.

"Good."

We move past the sign and follow a meandering gravel road until we reach the edge of a town that is absolutely, one hundred per cent, *not* charming.

From a distance, all I could see of Elston-Fright was a cluster of weatherboard houses, painted white and huddled together, with little roads snaking between them.

Up close, it's *very* different.

The houses here aren't actually painted white at all; they've just been bleached that way from years of sitting forgotten in the sun. And for every house with its lights on, there are two that have been left cold and empty. Some have their windows smashed in, jagged shards left like teeth in gaping mouths. Others have rusted car skeletons sitting out front.

And there's something else, too. Something I could never have sensed from all the way out on the rock-that-doesn't-exist. Dark secrets, humming in the air.

Witchcraft, simmering and seething underfoot.

How long have the Witches menaced this town? I

wonder. Just the thought of it makes my wax crawl. It's like I can feel them all around me, even though we left them behind on the rock-that-doesn't-exist.

What was it Old Man said about this place?

The Witches have spread a sickness over that town.

Is this what he meant, then? This heavy shadow that hangs over the town, was it left behind from all of the terrible spells the Witches have done? Years of bad magic and snatching kids for their own use...did it leave a poison in the streets of Elston-Fright?

"Why would anyone choose to live here?" I mutter.

I can't imagine growing up in a place like this. In all the times I've pictured my life – and there have been a lot of them – it never looked *anything* like Elston-Fright.

Right now, the streets are completely dead.

Everyone is bunkered down ahead of the storm.

Still, I'm careful to stay shielded from view, hidden in the shadow cast by a row of weeping peppermint trees, in case anyone happens to peek out their window.

But when I see a house with people moving about inside – the first fleshies I've seen in my entire death who *aren't* Witches – something wriggles in the place my tummy should be. I forget all about the fact I'm meant to be hiding. Before I know I'm doing it –

I dart across the road. Leap over their fence.

Click-click-click! Simon warns.

"Shush!" I say, as I tiptoe through the weed-filled garden bed.

I duck behind a shrub and peek through the fleshies' window, into an eggshell blue kitchen that has an old and clunky-looking stove taking up most of the far wall. A single table with spindly legs rests in the room's centre, with three chairs placed around it. In the corner, a fourth chair has been propped against the wall. One of its legs is hanging loose.

Click-click.

"Did we get caught spying on the Witches?" I remind him.

Click, he admits.

"Have we *ever* been caught spying on the Witches?"

...click.

"Exactly. So just trust me, will you?"

Then, I peer inside. "I want to see this."

Inside the kitchen, two women are moving about.

One of them has white skin, short pink hair and wears a jumper like knitted egg yolk. She is standing beside the stove, stirring something that bubbles and simmers.

It wafts through the gap in the window, spicy and warm.

The other woman has brown skin and wears a sage-coloured dress, lavender tights and bright cherry shoes. As I watch, she places three mismatched bowls around the table, swaying her hips and humming while she does it. And even though I don't know the song, I can't help but be reminded of Girl, and how she used to sing while she danced around our roof.

"How are they doing that?" I wonder out loud.

It's the strangest thing, but the little blue kitchen appears to be completely free from the Witches' dark magic. The rotten wickedness that hangs over Elston-Fright, it growls and snarls around the edges of the house, but never *quite* seems to reach inside.

I don't even think they know they're doing it.

The woman in the dress turns and wraps her arms briefly around the other, who beams. At that moment, the Witches' magic recoils further – like an anemone that's been poked with a stick. It makes an angry fizzing sound that nobody but me seems to notice.

Fizz. Fizz. Pop. Pop. Fizz.

It only lasts for a second, then the magic swarms back around the house. But again, it doesn't move past the walls.

(Seriously, how are they doing that?)

The woman in cherry shoes begins riffling through a drawer. She extracts three spoons, all with different handles, and sets them on the table. Then, three butter knives.

Just then a young boy walks in. He looks a lot like the woman in the cherry shoes, who twists towards him and plants a kiss right on top of his head.

And as she does, the darkness clinging to the house retreats again.

Fizz. Pop. Fizz. Fizz. Pop.

My hand rushes to my own seaweed hair. I touch the spot where I saw the woman kiss the boy and try to imagine what something like that might feel like.

Suddenly – and not for the first time – I wish I could Spook.

Spooking is the first of three Ghostly Acts – a special trio of powers, reserved just for the dead, that are *kind of like magic*. Except that unlike magic, you don't need a Spellspring to do them. And unlike magic, you can't learn them. As a ghost, you simply find yourself able to perform one – or, if you're lucky, two – of the Acts. I've never known a ghost who could do all three, but I have met plenty who couldn't do any at all.

The *first* Ghostly Act, Spooking, is the only way a ghost can communicate with fleshies. A ghost who can Spook is able to make leaves shake and wind chimes dance. They can stand behind a curtain and make it wrap around their ghostly form, taking their shape.

That part doesn't interest me much. I've already got this wax body, so I don't need to shake leaves or wear curtains. Being seen would be easy for me – if I wanted it.

It's the other part of Spooking that I wish I could do. Ghosts who can Spook are actually able to make their voices *heard* by fleshies.

I can't Spook. I can't perform the first Ghostly Act. The only Act I can do is the third.

If I *could* Spook, though, maybe I would crash through the door and join the family inside the little blue kitchen. Maybe I would grab the broken chair, fix it with a sticking spell and join them at the table. I wouldn't be able to eat anything...but who cares?

Just then, a niggling doubt creeps in. I try to ignore it, but it refuses to budge. Would a fleshie family even want a kid made of wax? *Yes,* I tell myself. *They would.*

Or at least, *my* family will. When I find them.

Because they have to...

...don't they?

The fleshie family sits down to eat. They ladle whatever is in the pot into the three bowls, then tear at bread and dip it into the soupy something. The boy has it all over his face in no time, and the woman with pink hair leans across the table to clean it from his cheek. He bats her hand away, and I can't help but feel angry at the boy.

(If I had a mother, I would *never* bat her hand away.)

Click-click-click-click-click!

Simon's warning pulls me from my thoughts.

I spin towards the road. "What?! Where?"

Click-click-click!

And then I see it.

Someone tall is coming along the road towards us. Moving quickly, in smooth and gliding strides, they're hidden beneath the hood of an oilskin coat like the ones I've seen the local fisherfolk wear on their boats. It reaches all the way to the ground.

What are they doing outside when a storm is on its way?

I tuck myself deeper into the shrub and watch the Fisher, trying not to move. Something inside me clenches up tight. The Fisher glides closer and closer.

Headed straight for us.

CHAPTER 8

The Fisher kept on gliding…

…gliding…

…gliding right past us.

Their oilskin made a *swooshing* sound as they passed the place where Simon and I were hiding. The Fisher reached the end of the street. Disappeared around the corner.

I felt the tense something inside me unclench.

"They didn't see us. Good."

Leaving behind the house with the blue kitchen wasn't easy. Even though I knew the clock was ticking – even though every passing second was taking us closer to the moment the Witches would land in Elston-Fright – I wanted to stay and watch them a bit longer.

I didn't, though.

With one last look towards their window, I slunk back onto the street, setting off again to find the Ungeneral Store – which, as it turns out, was quite simple.

All I had to do was follow the trail of witchcraft.

The dark and humming sickness that is spread across the town of Elston-Fright hangs like a stench, so all I had to do was follow it to where it grew most stinky. I hurried towards the place where the Witches' magic was thickest, feeling it turn heavy around me, pressing down from every angle. I pushed through it. Eventually it brought me here.

To the very centre of Elston-Fright.

The square is little more than a collection of dilapidated shopfronts. There's a sadness about it that settles under my wax skin and makes me feel all queasy. Some of the stores have been boarded up and abandoned entirely – forgotten, unwanted, and left for dead. Like the rest of Elston-Fright, the town's heart is withered and decaying.

Except for the store right in front of me, that is.

Sandwiched between Bram's Fish-and-Chip Shop and Mrs Marlin's Bait-n-Tackle sits an unmarked store that snaps and pops and fizzles with bad magic. Its midnight paint is glossy and perfect. Its big and spotless windows reflect the evening sky above in shades of pewter and silver and white. Brandished across them, in crisp gold paint, are four words.

The last two words shimmer differently to the others, and I get the strangest feeling that only some people are able to read them at all.

Woeful Wares?

I suddenly realize that I have absolutely no clue what business it is that the Merchant does with the Witches behind the doors of her Ungeneral Store. I have no idea what dark dealings go on here. Still, I know that's what this place is. It's the Ungeneral Store.

It has to be. It *reeks* of bad magic.

The store hums like a generator, almost like it's sucking the life from around it and leaving the town hollow. It couldn't be more different from the little blue kitchen from earlier, with the fleshie family who somehow seemed to be nudging the Witches' magic *out*.

Instead...the Ungeneral Store seems to draw the darkness *closer*.

Behind the store's window, teetering stacks of books sit on spindly-legged tables. Creepy porcelain dolls rest beside limp marionettes. There are towers of tarnished copper coins, no shortage of glass baubles and more brass doohickeys than I can count.

The lights are off inside. It's empty.

And the Witches aren't here yet.

(Good.)

Ignoring the uneasy feeling that's building inside me, I step nearer to the front door. Inside, on the far wall and at the back of the store, a spare key is dangling from a hook.

"There!" I say. "Do you see it, Simon?"

Click-click.

"Out of luck and out of reach," I start. I watch the key begin to wriggle and shake. It lifts itself from its hook. Hangs unsupported in the air. "You I need, you I beseech." The key starts floating through the air towards me. "Thing I seek, please come hither."

The key drops. Catches itself. Jerks about. Then finally, it halts. The key falls to the floor, and it starts to drag itself the rest of the way – closer and closer.

"Hurry now, don't you dither."

It slips under the door and into my waiting hand.

"Gotcha!" I say.

As I stand, an uncomfortable feeling washes over me. Like I'm being *watched.* It creeps up my back and over my shoulders, coming to a stop at the top of my head, where it makes my seaweed hair prickle. I peer behind me, half expecting to find the Fisher from earlier.

But there's nobody around at all.

I move quickly, sliding the key into the keyhole. The door unlocks smoothly. It swings open without a sound. I step inside, into a chill. It's only then that I realize I have no idea what I'm doing. I mean, I know *what* I'm looking for. Old Man told me. I just don't know *where* it is. And glancing around me now, I'm guessing that finding it isn't going to be easy.

"There's so much *stuff* in here," I whisper.

Click-click.

"Where do we even start?"

I move deeper into the cluttered store, passing fancy polished wardrobes with tarnished mirrors. Battered metal chests bolted shut like coffins. Mannequins with their noses chipped and eyes scratched off loom from a dark corner, arms outstretched.

All of it is creepy. But none of it is magical.

And then I notice the curtain.

Made of sapphire-coloured velvet, it sways even though there's no hint of a breeze inside the Ungeneral Store. Anyone else might be confused by a curtain that moves on its own, but not me. I know the whispers of magic when I see them. I hurry towards the curtain, move to push it aside...and it's as if the dancing velvet grips me by the arm.

"Wo-ARGH!"

It yanks me into the next room. A feeling like seasickness washes through me when the floor completely falls away. Upside down becomes right side up.

"Hold on, Simon!" I cry out.

I stumble backwards.

(Which is in actual fact forwards.)

The room keeps spinning and spinning.

When the world finally stops swirling around me, and I realize that I *am* in fact still standing upright, I hurry to ask Simon, "Are you all right?"

Click-click, he says.

Looking around me, the room we've stumbled into appears to be a perfect copy of the one we just left.

Well, it's *almost* a perfect copy. There are some… differences.

The mirrors in this room swim with shifting shadows not made by anything in the room around them. The old metal chests are not only bolted shut but bound in chains too. They shake and rattle and moan. And the mannequins in the corner –

I think that maybe they used to be *real* women. Taloned women, with crinkled skin and deep hollows under their cheeks. Empty sockets where their eyeballs should be. Mouths that are just big black circles lined with row after row of razor-sharp teeth.

Click-click? Simon asks.

I shake my head. "They're not alive."

(Still, I try not to glance at them again.)

"Let's get looking for it," I whisper to Simon.

I begin to move around room, ignoring the moaning and groaning that is coming from the chests. Most

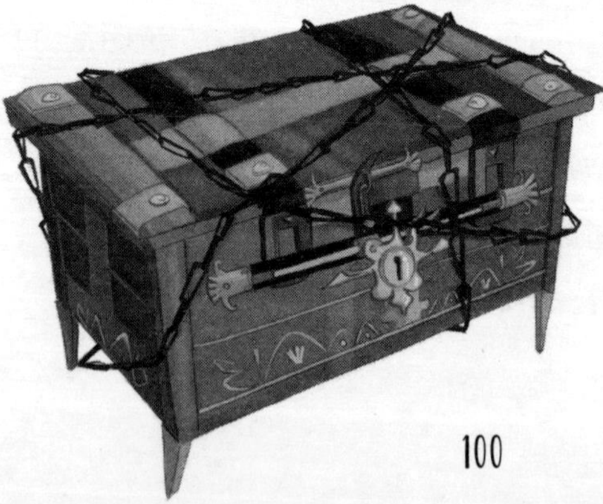

of the shelves in this room are lined with glass jars stuffed full of slimy-looking somethings swimming in a kind of oily stuff. I try not to think about what's inside them, but if I absolutely *had* to guess, I would say innards and teeth and earlobes.

"*Yuck,*" I say quietly.

In a way, I'm kind of reminded of my beachcombing missions with Simon, where we hunt for shells and other things left by the ocean. Except this time, we're hunting for the thing that will reunite me with my name and my memories and my family.

Click-click-click-click?

"Nothing yet."

Each shelf, I notice, has an old and yellowing label stuck on it. So does every drawer in this place, too. Each one bears a letter and a number, in curly handwriting.

"It's some kind of code," I say to Simon.

I cross the room, inspecting each of the labels and trying to work out what they might mean. On the labels along one side of the room, the code starts with the letter "E".

And along the opposite side, they begin with the letter "W".

Click! Simon realizes suddenly.

I nod. "East and West."

Click-click-click.

"Yep. And I bet those ones over there" – I point forwards – "have 'S' written on them." Then, I spin and point back in the direction we came. "And over there must be 'N'."

I move across the room to check.

And sure enough, I'm right.

"The numbers move from high to low, left to right. So then…the letter must tell you which side of the room to look. Then you find the numbered shelf or drawer."

I pause. Think. "But labelling all of them is only useful if…"

If there is a list or something.

"There!" I shout. "Simon, look!"

Near the sapphire-coloured curtain, on the bottom shelf of a tall counter topped with an old-fashioned cash register, rests a big old book. It's poking out at an odd angle, and it's all tattered and falling apart. Across its spine I can just make out three peeling words.

CATALOGUE AND DIRECTORY

I dart behind the counter. Crouch down.

"Simon!" A grin spreads across my face. An excited something ignites in my not-belly. "Everything in the store has a place. And that place is *labelled*."

I open the heavy book.

A few loose sheets of paper fall to the floor.

Scrawled across each of the book's pages, in faded ink, are all of the gruesome artefacts that the Merchant has ever held in the Ungeneral Store. Thousands of them, each one marked with its name, the date it was entered into the catalogue and *the place where it's kept*.

"And each item's place is listed in here!"

Simon clicks excitedly back at me.

"Which means that *it* might be in here, too."

The book is divided into sections. I flip right past "Trinkets and Talismans", ignore "Poisons and Potions", and head straight for the pages of "Biologics and Fleshes":

Butcher's Right Hand – c. 05 October 1971 – E.127
Finger of Bride Undead – c. 13 November 1977 – W.101
Liar's Tongue – c. 27 November 1982 – N.013

I don't remember exactly what year it is any more, but I know I didn't die *that* long ago. I flick forwards to the more recent entries, scanning the pages –

"Here it is!"

I find the item I'm looking for.

And tear the sheet from the book.

"Who is in my store?" comes an unfamiliar voice.

The shock of hearing it makes me cry out.

(Luckily, fleshies can't hear me.)

"I am closed for trade tonight." The voice is smooth, and the words are clipped. The voice is coming from somewhere behind me, on the other side of the curtain and near the shop's front door. The words are followed by a sound like a knife being unsheathed.

"And I do *not* take kindly to trespassers," the Merchant says.

Chapter 9

"In my Room of Woeful Wares, are you?" says the Merchant, and I can tell she's edging closer to the curtain now. "You are either very brave, or very foolish."

Click-click-click! Simon warns me.

I throw myself into a cupboard. It's ancient and musty, and I have to fold my body into a strange shape just to fit inside. I jam the door shut behind me, nearly bumping into a row of triangular-shaped bottles with silver necks and little teardrop stoppers. One threatens to topple right off its shelf, but I catch it just in time and hastily place it back, careful not to make a sound.

There's a string tied around its neck, with a tag dangling from it.

In curly handwriting, the tag reads:

BANSHEE-IN-A-BOTTLE
for trapping ghosts

(I suddenly wish I'd hidden somewhere else.)

"I do not pretend to know how you broke into my store," the Merchant says, her voice coming from inside the Room of Woeful Wares now. "But I do know – and think it only fair to inform you – that doing so was a catastrophic misstep on your part."

Her words cut like a razor blade. I dare to peek through the gap in the doors and do a double take. Because the Merchant doesn't look at all how I imagined.

Standing ramrod straight, she wears a crisp black suit that is sharp at its edges and pointy at its corners. Her blonde hair, cropped short like her words, is all wet and slicked back. Cunning eyes twinkle in the dim light. "Fine," she sighs to the room at large.

Then she shrugs. Sheathes her knife.

"Have it your way," she says.

The Merchant reaches into her jacket and extracts something tucked into her waistband. Whatever it is, it's long, white and forked like a giant letter "Y". It's cracked down its length but not yet broken. "We can play your little game," she tells me, "although you should know that if you will not come out on your own, I do have means to *draw* you out." She waves the forked thing in the air. "Have you seen one of these before?" she says.

Then, with a scoff, "No, I do not suppose you have."

Whatever the thing is, the Merchant grips both ends of it, with one prong in each hand. She points the longest fork right at the cupboard I'm hiding inside –

– but then directs it away from me.

The Merchant points the three-ended thing into each and every dark and shadowy corner in her Room of Woeful Wares, one at a time. "It is a divining bone," she continues, "which means that it can deliver its owner to any living thing that they may seek."

Grey-green light catches on her face. It's all sharp lines and shadows.

"Allow me to demonstrate," she says.

The Merchant raises the divining bone close to her lips and whispers to it, loud enough for me to hear: "Find me the thief who entered my store without invitation."

The divining bone begins to hum.

"*Whatever* they may be," the Merchant finishes.

That last part worries me. It's like she already suspects that I'm something other than just your average robber. I mean, not that I *am* a robber. Are you a robber if you take back something that was stolen from you in the first place? No, I don't think so.

But wait...did she say any *living* thing?

Relief floods through me, washing away the fear, only for a second though. Because just then the crack that runs the length of the divining bone lights up orange, like there's a fire trapped inside it. A wicked grin cuts across the Merchant's face.

"Well, well," she says. "There you are."

The Merchant has the divining bone pointed at my

hiding place and is stalking in my direction, mean eyes staring ahead. I back away from the doors, but it's pointless. It's not like there's anywhere for me to go. I'm trapped. And she's headed right for me.

None of this makes any sense. I'm not even alive!

So then how can the divining bone have…?

I hear the softest *click*.

"Simon!"

Before I can stop him, he jumps up and lands on the cupboard door. I make a grab for him, but he's already scampered away and scurried through the crack. I press my abalone shell eye up against it – "Simon, come back here!" – just as the Merchant's arms jerk upwards, yanked in Simon's direction by the divining bone as if it's drawn to him like a magnet.

Because it wasn't me the divining bone detected.

It was *him*.

"What are you, then?" the Merchant wonders aloud, looking up towards the ceiling, where Simon is running circles and zigzags and loop-the-loops to try to distract her. "A pesky little rock pixie, perhaps?" she says. "Or, no…a seafoam sprite?"

Then she narrows her eyes and licks her lips.

"Oh, I *do* hope it is the latter." Her eyes sparkle. "There is little I love more in this world than a meal of seafoam sprite and pickled samphire – on toast, naturally."

I burst from the cupboard, but too late.

Simon has already scurried across the ceiling and disappeared through the velvet curtain, back into the front room. The Merchant follows close behind.

"Got you!" she cries triumphantly.

"I'm coming, Simon!" I call out. "Hold on!"

This time, when I reach the velvet curtain, I anticipate the topsy-turvy of it all, and so when I'm spat out on the other side, I don't lose my balance.

"Let him go!" I shout.

Not that the Merchant hears me, obviously. She's a fleshie. Still, the sound of me crashing through the curtain – and nearly taking out a stack of books on this side of it while I'm at it – is enough to make her stop. The Merchant turns, her fist closed around Simon. She looks at me. Scrunches up her face. "And what are *you*?" she says distastefully.

I hurry to mutter the beckoning charm, and Simon zips straight out of the Merchant's grip. He flies through the air. Lands in my outstretched hands.

"You're okay," I promise him.

I tuck him into the pocket of my overalls.

Then button it shut nice and tight.

"I see," says the Merchant. "A Witch."

The hungry way she talked about pixies and sprites is gone. The Merchant says the word *Witch* like it's something to be scraped off her boot – which is weird, given her store is filled with evil magic stuff. She stalks towards me. "How many times have I told your master that he needs to make an appointment before sending one of you to my store?"

Then she pauses. Frowns.

Something passes behind her eyes that I don't quite recognize. She rests the divining bone on a nearby shelf and steps closer. Leans down until her nose is nearly touching my forehead. I'm about to do my fire hex when she says, "You do not *look* like any Witch I have ever met." Her hand races to something hanging around her neck.

Whatever it is, it starts to pulse under the fabric of her shirt.

"I assure you, Merchant," interrupts a rasping croak from somewhere over her shoulder, "that whatever this ramshackle creation is, it is most certainly *not* one of us."

I freeze all over.

Because this time, the voice is a familiar one.

With her jaw clenched, the Merchant spins to face the man standing in her doorway. His teetering and crumbling silhouette cuts against the night sky behind him.

"And yet here you are," she says, "not far behind."

The man stalks closer, a darkness clinging to his edges like smoke. I shudder when he begins to slink around me in a circle, eyeing me up and down with a scowl.

Up close, his hollowed-out eye sockets are even more horrible.

Up close, his every breath whistles and rattles.

Up close, Worst-Witch is terrifying.

Chapter 10

"It appears to be some kind of effigy," Worst-Witch says, talking about me. "Tragically amateur magic, performed by someone with only the most basic grasp on spells."

He steps closer. Leans over me.

I try my best not to shake.

My wax skin does crawl, though, when he runs a long and crooked finger up my arm and over my shoulder. He tugs at my seaweed hair. Sniffs his fingers and frowns. "I can only assume," he drawls, "that it was sent to steal something from your Ungeneral Store."

Then Worst-Witch flicks his wrist and –

SQUELCH!

– my feet are stuck to the floor.

"I'll dispose of it later," he says lazily.

(Like I'm some tiny nuisance.)

I try to lift my feet, but they won't budge. If Worst-Witch's magic was fading earlier, back when he tried to curse Gorflunk in the shack on the rock-that-doesn't-exist, it's *definitely* not faded any more. I guess the Witches must have brewed their malicewater just right. They must have guzzled it down and stretched their fading magic – for now, at least.

Worst-Witch turns his back on me.

I decide to take my chance.

The sticking spell that he just used on me is the same one that I use to stick and unstick the loose sheet of iron from the roof above their shack. It's the same one that I use to glue my eyes and my teeth and my hair into place. And so, I can easily say the un-spell right now. I can run away from this place. Only, when I glance back towards the doorway…

…two cormorants are already blocking the way out.

They waddle through the door – and as they do,

their bones begin to make crunching and snapping and popping sounds. Their legs grow longer, their feathers shrink away to nothing and their wings change into arms. Once they're done – once they've changed back into their fleshie forms – they take their places standing beside Worst-Witch.

He waves a hand towards the door.

It swings shut by magic.

SQUELCH!

We're trapped.

I brace myself to be melted into a puddle or blasted into pieces, but it doesn't happen. Instead – and just like Worst-Witch – Scraggleknee and Gorflunk act like I don't even exist. Like I'm something to be dealt with later. Instead, the Witches surround the Merchant.

"A displeasure to see you, Gorflunk," she says.

"Likewissse," comes his hissed reply.

The Merchant turns to Scraggleknee and pinches her nose. "I see you are still staging your one-man protest against bathing, Scraggleknee. Some things never change."

He scowls at her. "How Scraggleknee has missed

your jokes, Merchant dear. Tell me, will you still be laughing when you take your last breath?"

The Merchant's smile falters.

"*I* will handle this," Worst-Witch interrupts.

Scraggleknee steps back and bows. "Of course."

Worst-Witch starts to circle the Merchant like a shark. And when he speaks next, he lingers on every venom-laced word, basking in the moment and dragging it out. "Would you say, Merchant, that our working relationship has become...*strained* of late?"

The Merchant's eyes narrow. She doesn't reply.

Worst-Witch nods. "I would too."

He begins to circle in the other direction.

"Deceit and trickery will do that, I suppose," he says.

The Merchant lifts her chin. Stares straight ahead. Raises her eyebrows.

"I have no idea what you are talking about," she says.

Worst-Witch stops pacing. "Don't you?"

He reaches into his pocket and extracts a square of paper. "It would seem you have been busy today, Merchant. Your store closed. And your house *empty*."

The Merchant's head whips towards him. "You entered my home?"

Her eyes widen when she sees the paper in his hand.

"Missing something?" Worst-Witch asks her.

He waves the paper in the air, and it falls open to reveal the map from earlier, with its circles and crosses and arrows in red. I recognize the writing now. The word *WITCHES,* which is scrawled across the map about a hundred times, is written in the same curly handwriting as the labels that line the shelves and drawers in the Room of Woeful Wares. The same handwriting that I saw on the tag that was dangling from the banshee-in-a-bottle. The same handwriting that fills the Ungeneral Store's *CATALOGUE AND DIRECTORY.*

The map doesn't belong to the Witches after all, I realize.

It's *hers*. The map belongs to the Merchant.

"How *dare* you break into my house!" the Merchant snarls.

"We only went to reclaim that which rightfully belongs to us," Worst-Witch says. "But the treasure wasn't there, as I'm sure you know. Still, it was not a complete waste of our time. We found this map. This *proof* of your duplicitous intentions." He traces a skeletal finger over the word *WITCHES*. "I should have suspected you had ambitions of your own."

The Merchant stands up a little taller and draws her shoulders back. It's almost enough to distract you from the fact her knees have started shaking – but not quite.

"How long have you been plotting this betrayal?" Worst-Witch continues. "How long have you been searching Elston-Fright and its surrounds, looking for the place where we hide?" He shakes the map in her face. "How long have you been *hunting* us?"

"You are growing paranoid, Witch," the Merchant says.

But sweat has started to collect over her brow. Her neck has turned tense and stringy. I notice her eyes flit from one Witch to the next. "What interest would I have in finding *you*?" she sneers. "I see more than enough of the three of you as it is."

"Lies!" Scraggleknee accuses her. "You want our book!"

"You ssseek to take *Magikal Maledictionsss,"* Gorflunk says.

"Enough!" Worst-Witch shouts at them.

I decide to take my chance. While everybody is distracted, I say the un-spell – "Kcuts dna doog sgniht owt eseht ekam. Kcud a no si kaeb eht ekil. Tac no liat dna tab no sgniw. Enob no hself dna enots no ssom" – and my feet come unstuck from the floor. I bolt into a shadowy corner and tuck myself behind a pile of musty old sailcloths. Nobody sees me do it.

"Why would she want *Magikal Maledictions*?" I whisper.

Click-click, Simon replies.

I don't get it. I don't understand why the Merchant would be trying to find their book. Not that I really care. I'm only here to find the thing the Witches stole from me.

"What interest would I have in your spell book?" the Merchant says, as if reading my mind.

Worst-Witch steps nearer to her. He leans forward so that his face is pressed right up against hers. She flinches – but she doesn't cower. "I think you know," he says.

Something over the Merchant's chest wriggles.

It's the same thing that I saw just before the Witches arrived. Whatever it is, it's hanging around her neck and she has it tucked into her shirt. The Merchant steps back and away from Worst-Witch. She races to cover the thing with a hand. "That," she hisses, "is *mine*."

Worst-Witch raises his eyebrows. "Is it now?" he says. "Because as I recall, it was we Witches who crafted the locket in the first place. We Witches who extracted the required flesh from the child. We Witches who bound it in silver, and we Witches who—"

"—agreed to the deal," the Merchant snaps.

Her lips quiver at their edges but she continues: "It was *you Witches* who agreed to the terms of the deal. The locket belongs to me...fair and square."

Something in my not-chest aches.

The locket. The *treasure*.

"*Simon,*" I say. "That's it!"

Click-click?

"Around her neck," I tell him. "That's what we came for."

Which means the Witches were wrong about it being hidden somewhere in the Ungeneral Store. It isn't tucked away on some shelf between fossilized molars and pickled spleens after all. The Merchant kept it on her this whole time. She's wearing it right now.

My name and my memories are *right there*.

I try to use the beckoning charm on the locket...

...but it doesn't work.

It's too heavily magicked to beckon.

Click-click-click, Simon says, warning me not to jump out from my hiding place behind the sailcloths and snatch it from around her neck. And I know he's right.

I can't do that.

Not with the Witches right there.

And so, there's nothing I can do at all except watch on as Worst-Witch steps closer to the Merchant again. He towers over her, his rattling breath reminding me of a cold wind moving through the roof. "Your deal was dishonest," he says to her. "You had me believe you had grown...*sentimental*. You asked to keep only that once we were done. And so, I let you—"

"It was a trade," the Merchant snarls. "Not a favour."

Worst-Witch raises a hand.

His ember eyes flicker.

"Did you really think you would be able to fool me, Merchant? Did you truly believe I would not realize what the locket was? But when I came to you a moon ago and demanded to take it back, you told me it had been sold – for a price you couldn't refuse and to someone far away." Worst-Witch bares his blackened gums. "That lie was your fatal mistake. After all, hadn't you told me the locket was so precious that you could never part with it?"

A bead of sweat rolls down the Merchant's jaw.

"I knew in that moment that you were trying to *hide* the locket from me," Worst-Witch says. He raises the map. "But it took until tonight to know for certain why."

Like a flash, the Merchant tries to swipe the map from Worst-Witch's grip –

– but he pulls his hand away just in time, still clutching it.

The Merchant's fist closes in mid-air.

"I think not," Worst-Witch says to her, folding the map and tucking it back into his pocket. He eyes the thing that's hanging around her neck. "I suspected the locket would be here in your store." A sneer. "I never imagined you would be so foolish as to *wear* it."

He reaches for it, bony fingers flexing on the air.

"Give the locket to me," he demands.

"*No.*"

"Then I will have to take it myself."

"We had a *deal,*" the Merchant repeats. "The locket was mine to keep. I played my role in its creation, too. Or have you forgotten about that?"

Worst-Witch waves her words away.

"A small effort," he says.

Worst-Witch points a finger towards a length of rope that hangs from a wall. It uncoils itself, snakes through the air and wraps around the Merchant.

It binds her tightly.

"What is this?" says the Merchant. "How dare—"

"Take our visit as a warning," Worst-Witch interrupts her, "that while you may trade in magic,

Merchant, it is only we Witches who wield it." He leans forward and lifts the locket from around her neck. Lumpy and uneven, it thumps in his grip like flesh.

(Which, under the silver, is exactly what it is.)

"And it will only *ever* be we Witches who wield it," he adds.

The Merchant struggles against the ropes.

"Let me go this instant!" she shouts.

But Worst-Witch isn't even paying her attention any more. Instead, he's gazing greedily at the locket in his hand. He caresses it with his thumb. A crooked grin cuts its way across his face when he lowers the chain over his head. As soon as the silver touches his skin...

...a fiery glow blazes in his empty eye sockets.

It burns red-hot for a moment, then fades. Smoke rolls from his hollowed-out eyes. He turns to the other two Witches. "Ours," he says triumphantly.

"You mean *mine*," I growl.

Click-click, Simon warns me.

But seeing the locket around Worst-Witch's neck makes me feel something like seasick. I watch it pulse, my memories coursing through it like blood, and I can't shake the thought that right there, beneath the locket's silver shell, are my name and the faces of my family. I unfold the piece of paper I tore from the *CATALOGUE AND DIRECTORY*.

Heart of a Child – c. 02 August 2010 – not for sale

CHAPTER 11

The Witches don't stick around for long. Scraggleknee and Gorflunk spend a few confused minutes looking for me – under tables, behind chairs and inside chests – before Worst-Witch announces that they should return to the rock-that-doesn't-exist at once.

"The wax effigy is of no consequence," he says.

"Of coursssse, Masssster," Gorflunk agrees.

But one of Scraggleknee's clawed and carbuncled hands is already clutching at the edge of the sailcloth that I'm hiding behind. He has a big fistful of it bunched up in his grotty grip, just a few centimetres in front of my abalone shell eyes. My whole body is rigid –

almost like I'm made of glass instead of wax. I try not to move.

Scraggleknee lets go of the sailcloth. "As you wish," he says reluctantly.

And my body unclenches.

Gorflunk and Scraggleknee move to Worst-Witch's side, pausing only to snarl at the Merchant, who is still struggling against the ropes and shouting to be released.

"You *beasts*!" she says. "We had a deal!"

Worst-Witch acts as if he can't even hear her. He unsticks the door with an un-spell and strides right on through it, back out into the night – wearing *my* heart.

The other Witches follow close behind him, sneering and cackling.

"Come back here!" the Merchant shouts after them.

They don't though. Of course not.

Then they're gone.

I slip out from my hiding place.

"Strange little wax person!" the Merchant says, wriggling in the ropes. Straining against them. "There you are. You know spells. I know you do. I *saw* it. Unbind me now."

I don't know the un-spell, though.

And even if I did, it's not like I'd help her. Not after she tried to hurt Simon. No, we're all safer with the Merchant tied up. And so instead, I ignore her and edge closer, my gaze locked on the thing resting beside her. On the Woeful Ware sitting on the shelf.

"I will give you whatever trinket you came here for," the Merchant bargains.

(She doesn't know the thing I'm after is already gone.)

"Just unbind me," she orders. "*Now.*"

I snatch up the divining bone. Turn. Run.

"Not that!" the Merchant shouts. "That belongs to me!"

But I'm already halfway towards the front door.

"Come back here!" the Merchant shouts. "Come BACK!"

I topple out of the door. Behind me, the Merchant continues yelling and cursing. The streets are empty, the Witches gone already. Still, I know we can catch them if we hurry. "It's okay," I tell Simon, unbuttoning my pocket with my free hand and placing him back on my shoulder. "We'll find them. Take it back. I have a plan. I'd die before I let them keep it."

Click-click-click.

"Yes, Simon, I do realize I'm already dead."

Click-click.

"It's called a figure of speech."

I grip the divining bone with both hands, and immediately it starts to hum. Holding it out in front of me, like I saw the Merchant do back in her Room of Woeful Wares, I spin on the spot. I point it towards each dark street that forks away from the town centre.

"Take me to the Witches," I instruct the bone.

At first nothing happens, and I worry that maybe ghosts can't work the thing. That perhaps the divining bone can only be controlled by the living – just like it can only *find* the living. But then its orange light crackles and sparks, coming to life. A jolt of something powerful runs through my arm. It tugs me in the direction of a dark side street.

"They went that way," I tell Simon. "Let's go."

And we hurry after them.

Forwards. Right. Forwards. Left. The divining bone leads us closer to the Witches.

(Or at least, I *hope* that's where it's leading us.)

The rain has arrived now – *splat, splat, splat, splat, splat* – and I know the storm won't be far behind. There's a rumbling in the distance, growing louder. "We need to catch the Witches before they change," I explain to Simon. "That will be our best chance."

Click-click-click.

"Exactly."

To cross the water and return to the rock-that-doesn't-exist, the Witches will first need to find three creatures that can either swim or fly. But even with the malicewater racing through their veins and boosting their magic, it's a spell that takes time. It takes time for their bodies to twist and bend and buckle. Time for them to grow fur or feathers or scales. For their mouths to become beaks or suckers or snouts. Their fingers to turn into claws or flippers or fins.

And that will give me enough time to do my sticking spell.

I'll glue the Witches in place. Swoop in while

they're stuck halfway between person and animal. I'll take back my heart and escape before they know what hit them.

CLICK! Simon says suddenly.

And I duck into a gap.

"What are *they* doing here?" I hiss.

I peek back around the corner. Prowling down the street towards us is the figure from earlier. The one in the oilskin. The Fisher. They glide without making a sound, dark as the night. And if Simon hadn't warned me, I probably would have run straight into them.

They turn another corner and disappear.

"Do you think they saw us?"

Click-click.

I wait until I'm sure they're not coming back, then step out from my hiding place. Ignoring the divining bone, I turn and head in the opposite direction to the way the Fisher went, trying to put some distance between us and them. More than once, I look back to check we're not being followed. Then the divining bone starts growling and shuddering again.

"I think the Witches are close," I tell Simon.

We turn another corner, arriving in a grotty back alley filled with overflowing rubbish bins that stink of fish guts and spew. Underneath that, something yeasty and fruity and rotten. The only light comes from the handful of street lights that haven't been smashed in yet.

"There they are!"

I slip into shadow and hurry closer.

The Witches are gathered together, staring up and pointing at something hidden. I can barely make out a handful of fuzzy and damp-looking bats, hanging upside down and hiding from the rain. "Not ideal," Worst-Witch says to the others, "but they will have to do."

He turns to Gorflunk. "You do it."

"Yesss, Masssster," Gorflunk says.

And then Gorflunk raises his hands. Magic begins to gather around them. I can't hear the words of the spell from here, but I see his lips move as he says them. His glowing purple eyes are locked on the bats.

Just then, something beyond the Witches catches my eye.

The Fisher.

Gliding swiftly towards the Witches from the other direction is the figure in the oilskin coat. The Witches don't even see them coming. In a flash, the Fisher is on them. And in one swift movement –

– the Fisher rips my heart from around Worst-Witch's neck.

Worst-Witch teeters. He grabs at Gorflunk's hair, who in turn clutches hold of Scraggleknee's robes. The three of them topple to a pile on the ground.

"Get off me!" Worst-Witch says. "Catch the thief!"

But the Fisher is fast. They've already slipped around another corner and disappeared with my heart. I race after them. In a single stride, I leap over the Witches…

…and a bony hand catches me around the ankle.

It brings me crashing down and I fall flat on my face. The divining bone clatters to the ground beside me, where it breaks clean in two.

(And in the chaos, the bats take flight.)

"You again?!" Worst-Witch spits at me.

I do the sticking spell faster than I've ever done it before – *SQUELCH! SQUELCH! SQUELCH!* –

sticking the Witches' feet to the ground, just like Worst-Witch did to me back in the Ungeneral Store. And then I jump back up. Before any of the Witches have a chance to say the un-spell, I snatch up the pieces of the divining bone and dart forwards.

"The effigy isss a *Witch*?!" says Gorflunk from behind me.

"Catch it!" crows Worst-Witch.

I turn the corner where I saw the Fisher disappear a moment ago, but they've vanished. Behind me, I know the Witches have done the un-spell because I hear them scramble to their feet. Still, I don't look back to check.

I just run.

The storm has well and truly hit by the time I stop. Overhead, the night sky dances with blasts of dazzling white sheet lightning. Cracks of thunder shake the air around me, and rain pelts down like bullets. "I think we'll be safe here," I tell Simon.

(He has taken cover in my hair again.)

Don't ask me what made me come to this place. I just did. Call it ghost instinct, but while I was running from the Witches, I saw this place in the distance and knew that if Simon and I could make it here, we would find protection from the storm. It was like there was a fish hook stuck in the place where my belly button should be, and at the other end of a long wire was this place, tugging me towards it. I followed that tugging feeling along a dark and winding path that led away from Elston-Fright, all the way here.

The gate is locked, though.

And so, I have to scramble over the fence.

When I land on the other side, I know straight away that my suspicions about this place were right. The moment my feet touch the earth, some familiar force reaches up out of the ground to welcome me. I don't bother asking Simon whether he feels it too – I know he doesn't. But I also know that I'm right about this place. It wants to take care of us.

Maybe cemeteries always side with the dead.

Ahead of us is a sprawling mass of higgledy-piggledy headstones. As soon as I reach them, the deathly energy that is fizzing through me grows even stronger. It seeps up out of the ground, making my entire body tingle. My seaweed hair starts to curl and uncurl.

It feels like every ghost who has ever called Elston-Fright Cemetery home has left a kind of

imprint behind. Whispers of who they were. Echoes of their abilities. The ghosts themselves are long gone, moved on to Death Proper, but I can still sense them.

This place makes me feel so much…more.

More powerful. More *ghostly*.

Click-click?

"Come on," I say.

Right in the very centre of the cemetery is an old and crumbling groundskeeper's shed, and it's that shed which I head towards now. I weave between the rows of stone slabs, all of them forgotten and overgrown with weeds, until Simon and I reach it. Built from thick and solid limestone, the shed's door is hanging from its hinges. I duck inside, to where it's cramped and musty and cold. But at least it's dry. "Let's get you warm," I say to Simon.

Click-click.

I find an old metal bucket and throw any tool I can find with a wooden handle into it. Hand spades. A small axe. Funny little fork things. I douse the whole lot in kerosene from a busted-up jerrycan, then bring to life a tiny flame at the end of my index finger.

I lean forwards.

SHWOOSH!

Fire leaps up. Scorches the ceiling.

Curling black smoke explodes from the bucket.

Immediately, my skin begins to soften.

I scurry back, away from the heat, and settle beneath the shed's only window. The moonlight that pours through it is dirty and dull. Rain splatters on the glass. Simon moves down my neck, over my shoulder and leaps to the floor. He hurries over to the bucket.

"There you go."

Click-click, he says appreciatively.

Simon curls up beside the fire, and for a while, everything is quiet except for the sounds of the storm raging and the flames crackling. In the silence, all I can think about is how *none* of what just happened adds up. Not one bit of it. I try to make sense of it but can't. Who is the Fisher? And what do they want with my heart? It's pretty clear they're not on the Witches' side, and so does that mean they're working with the Merchant? If they are…

…I don't understand why.

Why does the Merchant want my heart in the first place? Why did she lie to the Witches about it? What does *any* of it have to do with *Magikal Maledictions*?

And then there's the question of my heart itself.

It's a question that's been scratching away at the back of my not-brain since I first overheard the Witches talking about it. About how it can *reunite them with magic*. Because if there really is a memory inside my heart that can lead them to a new Spellspring…

…does that mean I knew about magic when I was alive?

I shake my head. There *must* be some piece still missing. Something I can't see. An invisible thread that will tie all these things together and help it make sense.

"Don't worry," I tell Simon. "I have a plan."

But he doesn't reply. If I listen carefully, I think I can hear a gentle string of *click-click-click*s coming from where he rests by the fire. He's fallen asleep.

"I have a plan," I mutter again.

(This time to myself.)

Only, I don't.

Not at all.

Chapter 12

Elston-Fright Cemetery sits on a cliff, high above the angry ocean. Since Simon is fast asleep, I decide to slip out of the shed. I make my way over to the cliff edge and sit down.

Then I just stay out here for ages.

I let the rain pour over me and soak through my overalls. It beads on my skin and rolls away, dripping off my toes and disappearing into the darkness. Way down below me, waves thrash and crash against jagged rocks – rocks that would crush the bones of any fleshie who accidentally stepped too close to the edge. And to my left, the lighthouse looms.

its shadow dances with each fresh blast of lightning.

I don't know how long I sit here exactly, but it must be past midnight by the time the rain stops and the clouds roll away. The sky clears to reveal a blanket of stars, with even the tiniest of them fighting for attention. The heavy and swollen moon hangs in the middle of them all, its edges clear and crisp and sharp. Bathed in its light, and way out to sea, is the rock-that-doesn't-exist. Even from here, I can see the ocean crash up and over its tide pools.

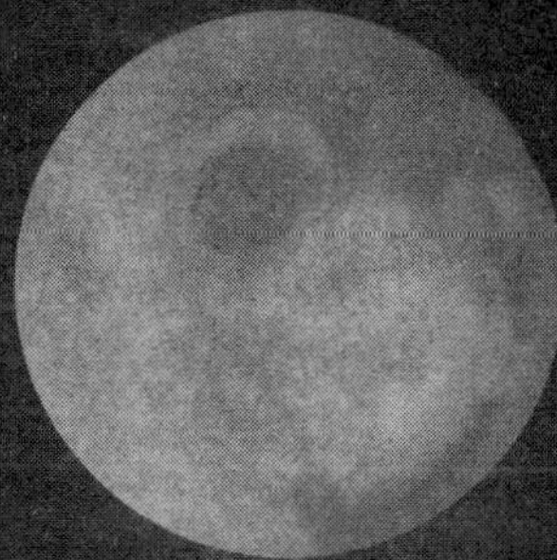

Between my fingers is the lucky black button.

I roll it back and forth, remembering the day that I first found it. I was on one of my beachcombing missions across the tide pools when I stumbled across it – something wedged into a narrow crack. It was small and black and perfectly round. A button.

Somehow, I knew straight away that I had seen it before.

Not during my death, maybe.

But in my *life*.

Don't ask me how I knew, exactly. I just did. Even without my memories – even without a brain to speak of – it's like some *other* part of me recognized it. Some invisible part of me started to hum the moment I picked it up. The air crackled all around me. I knew right away that the button must have belonged to me when I was a fleshie kid. I knew I must have dropped it, back on the day the Witches first brought me to the rock-that-doesn't-exist.

I knew that the button had sat there for years…

…waiting for me to find it again.

Anyway, I didn't *just* bring the button with me tonight because it's lucky. I brought it because I thought that once Simon and I had found my heart – once it had led me back to my family – that I would simply pluck the button from my pocket and show it to them. Immediately, they would remember which jacket or cardigan or shirt the button had belonged to. They would know it was me, even if I *do* look different to how they remember.

But there goes that plan.

For some reason, my abalone shell eyes start to prickle and sting.

A drop of water leaks out from behind one of them. I hurry to dab it away, then tuck the button back into my pocket and forget about all that…all that stuff.

Because I am *not* the kind of ghost who lets her eyes leak.

The shards of the divining bone are sitting next to me. I've already tried fixing them with a sticking spell, but it was useless. They're broken beyond repair. No spell will help. Just like my heart couldn't be beckoned from around the Merchant's neck, the bone can't be repaired now. Even in pieces, it's too heavily magicked. I collect the shards.

"Where is the Fisher?" I ask them.

(Nothing.)

"*Who* is the Fisher?"

(Still nothing.)

I shake the pieces of the divining bone.

Bash them against the cliff edge. "Tell me where they are!"

But of course, none of that helps even a little bit.

Eventually, I tuck the pieces back into my overalls and stand up. I need to tell Simon the truth, I've decided – that there is no plan, that I shouldn't have let him come with me in the first place and that all of this is my fault. But when I turn around to make my way back towards the groundskeeper's shed, I nearly jump clean out of my wax skin –

– when I come face to face with a fleshie boy.

He's just standing there, right in front of me.

Staring.

I feel myself freeze. It's like my entire body has been struck with a sticking spell or something. I urge my legs to move – to *run* – but they refuse to do it.

It takes me a moment to realize the boy is talking.

"What are you?" he asks.

The boy is a little taller than me, but I'm guessing he must be about the same age as I was when I was snatched. He's got white hair, silver eyes and skin so pale that it glows blue in thc moonlight. His striped pyjamas are a bit too short for him, so his ankles poke out from their bottoms, and he's wearing fuzzy slippers.

"Let me guess," he continues, "some sort of merperson?"

The boy takes a step closer.

Then another. He raises his chin.

And then he looks down his nose at me suspiciously.

"Where's your *tail?*" he says. "How come you're out of the water? Why were you sitting around in the cemetery in a storm? It's *very* strange merperson behaviour."

That's when I realize what I need to do.

"Moss on stone and flesh on bone," I begin.

(Is it just me, or does the boy look at me funny?)

"Wings on bat and tail on cat," I continue.

I eye his slippers and prepare to direct the first of two sticking spells at them. I'll glue them to his feet, then rush through the spell again, sticking the slippers' soles to the ground beneath them. I'll trap the boy in place, like I did to the Witches back in that grubby back alley. Just as it bought me enough time to run away from them, the same trick should give me enough time to bolt back to the shed, collect Simon and get out of here.

"What's that?" the boy asks. "Some sort of poem?"

His question stops me halfway through my spell.

"I don't really like poems," he continues. "I prefer stories. Adventure ones. But as long as your poem isn't all soppy and gross, I'll listen to it. What's it called?"

My magic sputters out. "Can you...hear me?"

(Now he is *definitely* looking at me funny.)

His face is scrunched up into a frown.

"Of course I can," he says. "Got two ears, haven't I?"

Even in the moonlight, I can tell he starts blushing the moment the words leave his mouth. His eyes flit from one side of my earless head to the other. "I didn't mean to offend," he starts, fumbling over his words. "It's totally fine *not* to have ears."

Then his shoulders drop.

"I'm sorry," he says, the words tumbling out of him. "It's just that I don't meet many people and – wait, are you people? Are you a person? What *are* you?"

I hear myself say, "Do you *always* ask so many questions?"

The boy beams.

"Yes," he says, matter-of-factly.

It feels strange – scary, even – to be talking to a fleshie. But what's weirder is that I don't really know *how* I'm doing it. The only way a ghost can talk to fleshies is by performing the first Ghostly Act, Spooking. But I *can't* do the first Act. I can't Spook...

...can I?

As if in response, the night air swells and shrinks around me. It tickles my hair and whispers to me like a friend. I glance back towards the rows of graves and realize that I *can* Spook – at least, I can while I'm here in the cemetery. It must be the concentration of death in this place that's letting me do it. The cemetery's energy – the memories of the once-ghosts who have been here – floods through me. The cemetery supercharges my ghostliness.

It's helping me perform the first Ghostly Act.

"I'm Flip," he says. "Flip Little."

I notice that he has his hand held out in front of him, like he's waiting for me to do something with it. It hangs there in mid-air. "You're meant to shake it," he explains.

I don't do it.

"As in with *your* hand," he says.

I stare back at him.

The boy called Flip doesn't *seem* dangerous in his too-small pyjamas and slippers, but you never know with these things. Flip blushes again. His arm drops to his side. "Is it just *my* hand you don't want to shake? Or is handshaking not something that merpeople do?"

I'm not sure what makes me say it.

"I'm not a merperson," I say. "I'm a ghost."

"Oh," he says. "Is that all?"

Flip looks unbothered, like he meets ghosts all the time. "I've never seen a ghost like you before," he says. "Well, I've never *seen* a ghost at all. Usually, I just hear them."

It takes me a moment to realize what Flip said. "Wait…are you saying that you've spoken to other ghosts? Here, in this cemetery?"

He nods.

"But how?"

He shrugs. "Sometimes they choose to be heard."

"You mean they Spook you?"

(*Like I am now*, I think.)

Flip's face scrunches up – like he's considering my question.

"Not really," he says eventually. Flip puffs out his chest and beams. "But not much can spook me, great-grandson of the last Lightkeeper."

"The last…what?"

"Lightkeeper!" Flip repeats. He thumps his chest with pride. "Warden of the lighthouse, guardian of Elston-Fright and protector against the evil magics that try to harm it."

Chapter 13

Flip convinces me to sit down and talk. "It'll be like having a friend," he says.

And so that's where we are now.

With our backs resting against a pair of headstones, Flip explains to me that Lightkeepers exist all over the world, stationed in corners where darkness gathers. "Nan says there are pockets on this earth where bad magic likes to collect, and that Elston-Fright is one of them. Us *Littles*," he says, emphasizing his name, "have been here almost as long as the town. We built the lighthouse, and we've lived in it ever since."

"You live in the lighthouse?"

I'd always thought it was abandoned.

Flip nods. He tells me that the lighthouse was never designed to guide ships or anything like that. Instead, he explains that its one job is to warn the town whenever evil magic comes to visit. "Kind of like a really big security alarm. In case Scallywaves or the Thundercurrent make their way here again." I see him shiver when he adds, "Or the Poltergusts."

Scally-whats? Thunder-huh?

And *Poltergusts?*

I want to ask Flip what they all are. Instead, I find myself saying something else entirely. "Well, no offence, but your lighthouse is *not* doing a very good job."

"What do you mean?"

"The Witches."

Flip stares at me, and his mouth falls open. His silver eyes widen like big coins. "Are you telling me there are *actual* Witches? Right here in Elston-Fright?"

I nod. "Horrible ones."

Flip is acting as if Witches are something to get really excited about, rather than what they actually are

– something to fear. "That's so cool," he breathes. "It's *really* bad, too, but still…Witches! How many are there? Does the town know about them? What do they look like? Where do they live? Has anybody tried to stop them? Ha—"

"They're hidden," I interrupt. "Nobody knows about them."

(He really does ask *so* many questions.)

Flip wants to know more about the Witches, so I tell him what I know. Not everything, obviously. I don't tell him about my heart. Just the other stuff, like how there are three of them, and how they must have been around for ages because the shadows of their magic linger on the air in Elston-Fright. I tell him that they live way out on the rock-that-doesn't-exist.

When I mention that last part, Flip asks me to show him where it is. He says that he's never read about a secret rock out to sea in his great-grandad's journals.

And so, I point to it.

"That's not a secret!" he says. "I can see it, clear as anything." But then, as soon as he turns away from it: "Wait, can you show me where the rock is again?"

I smirk. "Told you."

"I bet they must have arrived in Elston-Fright *after* the lamp in the lighthouse went out," Flip says. "Because my great-grandad doesn't talk about them anywhere in his journals. And I'd know, because I've read every single page. Some of them *twenty* times."

"What do you mean the lamp went out?" I ask.

Flip shrugs. "It just stopped working one day," he tells me. "Nan says the Light betrayed us Littles. She says it turned its back on us after her dad died."

He shakes his head. "I've *tried* telling her I can fix it, because I'm really good at fixing stuff, but she won't even let me near the lantern room. Keeps it locked up. Nan says that all that stuff...that it ended when great-grandad died. She calls him the last Lightkeeper and says we don't need another one, since nobody really believes in magic any more."

"You live with your nan?" I ask. "Don't you have parents?"

Flip's face falls and the sparkle leaves his eyes.

(Straight away, I wish I hadn't asked.)

"They're dead," he says. "Both of them."

I shift about on the ground, suddenly uncomfortable.

"They worked on the wharf," he explains. "Fisherfolk, like everybody else around here. Then one day, when I was a baby, they were swept away and never found."

His face turns dark.

"It was a Scallywave," he says, "and it never would have happened if there was a Lightkeeper. Anyway, it's just been me and Nan since then. She's cool, I guess. Just scared of lots of stuff. She doesn't like me leaving the lighthouse, not even for school. Nan says it's safer if she teaches me. Only, she's a rubbish teacher and so I have to teach myself, mostly. Luckily my dad had *loads* of books, so I read those and..."

I let him keep talking.

But I've stopped listening.

Whenever I imagined fleshie families, they all looked like the one in the house with the little blue kitchen. They were happy and full and untouched by dark magic. I'd never really stopped to think that there might be living kids with dead parents.

It reminds me of something Girl said to me, right

before she slipped away into Death Proper. She told me that things don't always look the way you imagined them.

She said *family* doesn't always look the way you imagined it.

I guess this is what she meant, then.

It still feels strange, talking to Flip like this. And maybe I shouldn't be doing it at all. It's just that…well, I haven't spoken to a fleshie my entire death, have I?

Also, talking to Flip has given me an idea.

Because if Flip really *does* know as much about the magic that collects here in Elston-Fright as he says he does, then there might still be time for me to come up with a plan after all. Maybe – *just* maybe – Flip might know where to find a new source of magic, running underground. He might know where to look for some seam of shiny, sparkly stuff that I can draw fresh magic from. He might know where I can find the second Spellspring.

Not that my magic seems to be running out.

Not like the Witches' has been.

(It's *very* odd.)

"So how come you're not invisible?" Flip asks.

I realize he is pointing at my seaweed hair and my wax toes.

"I'm made of all this stuff because I Possessed it," I say.

Flip's eyes light up. "Ghosts can possess things? That's so cool!"

"Not all ghosts," I say, shaking my head. "I can though."

I explain to Flip that I first found the instructions for building a body made of wax when the Witches left *Magikal Maledictions* open to a page about something called effigies.

"But since I didn't have hands or anything," I say, "I had to learn other spells first. I learned a beckoning charm, to collect the wax from their candles. And a sticking spell, to glue the other stuff in place. It took years to get everything right, and once I was done…"

I tell him how I used Possession to pour myself into it.

Possession. The *third* Ghostly Act.

"That's awesome," Flip says. His eyes are so wide now, they might fall out of his sockets. "Are there other Ghostly Acts? Other cool ghost powers you can do?"

"There are three."

I explain that the first Ghostly Act, Spooking, is how I'm talking to him right now. That with Spooking, ghosts can lift sheets over themselves or make curtains shake. They can make their voices heard. I tell him that normally I can't Spook at all.

"I think maybe the cemetery is helping me do it," I say.

He nods. "Is there a second Act, then? If Spooking is the first one and Possession is the third, there must be a second one in between them, right? Wait, let me guess...laser fingers! No, *lightning* fingers! Is that it? Can you shoot electricity out of your fingertips?"

"It's Flight."

He snaps his fingers. "That was going to be my next guess."

"I can't Fly, either," I add – before he asks.

If I *could* Fly, I never would have been stuck on the rock-that-doesn't-exist. If I could Fly, I would have zipped over the waters and come to Elston-Fright years ago.

Which is confusing...because Girl *could* Fly.

With eyes like topaz and skin that crackled with tiny sparks of electricity, Girl was forever swooping between the rafters of our roof, or else soaring high above the rock-that-doesn't-exist – when she wasn't daydreaming and chatting to the ocean, that is.

Which she did a *lot*.

But she never left. She stayed on the rock with me until Death Proper took her.

Girl could Spook, too. She was one of those ghosts who was able to do two of the Ghostly Acts. She may not have been any good at magic – I did *try* to teach her, except she never managed a single spell – but she was good at the first and second Acts.

Especially the second one.

"Go on," Flip says, pulling my mind away from the rock-that-doesn't-exist and dragging it back to my present, here in Elston-Fright Cemetery. I hadn't realized he was still talking. "So you built an effigy and Possessed it. After that, you found those overalls and – *boom!* – you became sort of like a kid again, only made of wax? That's so cool!"

I pause. "Something like that."

The truth is that it was Girl who found these overalls, not me. She saw them downstairs in the Witches' shack one day. Neither of us knew where they had come from, but Girl really liked them. She asked me to beckon them up into our roof for her – so, I did.

It was the biggest thing I had *ever* beckoned.

After that, Girl used the overalls to practise her Spooking. Using the first Ghostly Act, she would breathe life into the overalls, make them wrap around her ghostly shape, and wear them almost as if she was made of something more than spectral nothingness. It took her a while to get Spooking right, but after she did, she was forever whirling and twirling around our roof in her overalls. It only ever lasted a few minutes though. Without a body…

…the overalls would just fall to the floor in a pile.

I don't tell Flip any of that stuff, though.

Because those memories are just for me.

Instead, I take my chance.

I ask him, "What's in your great-grandad's journals?"

Flip beams, and I think he's glad to talk about the last Lightkeeper again. "All kinds of stuff! Every monster or weather ghoul that's ever found its way here."

I nod. "And what about Spellsprings?"

"Spell-*whats*?"

"Springs," I repeat.

Flip looks at me blankly.

"They're special places," I explain. "Full of magic."

"What kind of places?"

"Anything, I think," I tell him. "A mountain, maybe? Or a cave?"

His face is all screwed up in concentration.

"...Maaaaybe," he says eventually.

And then his eyes light up. "You want to come and check? The journals are heavy, but Nan sleeps like a shipwreck and I'm sure I can sneak you into the lighthouse. We can see if there's anything in the journals about your...your Spellsprings."

I glance back towards the shed. I can't leave Simon there.

But I *can* bring him with me.

I nod to Flip.

"I'll meet you there," I promise.

I watch Flip long enough to see him disappear into the forest, headed back to the lighthouse. Then, I turn and bolt for the groundskeeper's shed. I can't wait to tell Simon about Flip and the journals. I can't wait to tell him about my plan to find the second Spellspring.

Hurrying towards the shed, zigzagging between graves, I spring over knotted mounds of grass as I go. There's no light coming through the shed window. I guess the coals from the fire I lit earlier have extinguished themselves by now. I leap over the top of a final row of headstones and land roughly on the ground. Jump back to my feet. Dart forwards.

I duck back inside…

…then stop.

The inside of the shed is a total mess. The bucket has been knocked over and there's ash all over the floor. A few coals remain. They glow dully. The shelves along the wall are all crooked and collapsed, and in the middle of the chaos sits a round critter the size of a cat, but with a face like a too-big mouse. Its eyes and nose are pink, and its fur is grey. Except for its curling tail, that is, which is white.

A possum.

"Simon?" I say, even though I can't see him anywhere. "Simon, who is this?" And then, when there's only silence, I look straight at the possum. "Who are you?"

It doesn't reply.

A creeping sense of dread crawls up over my shoulders. "Have you seen my friend Simon?" I ask it, nervous now. "He's a spider. Eight legs. Kind of furry, like you."

The critter just stares blankly back at me. It's got evil eyes for a possum, all beady and mean. Its nails are too long and curled. They're sort of yellow. And its fur, I realize now, is all folded over itself in a way that is definitely not normal for a possum.

A wriggly and jointed something pokes out from its mouth.

"No!" I jump forwards and make a grab for the possum, but it ducks out of the way just in time and I miss. "No!" I shout again. "Let him go!"

The possum swallows Simon.

Then it grins like a Witch.

Chapter 14

"Out of luck and out of reach," I mutter, saying the magic words faster than I ever have before, my hands outstretched towards the possum-that-is-in-actual-fact-a-Witch.

How could I have left Simon behind in the shed?

"You I need, you I beseech."

That ugly, overgrown tree rat. They're not even supposed to *eat* spiders. Possums are meant to be herbivores. "Thing I seek, please come hither."

But of course, this possum *isn't* a possum.

"Hurry now, don't you dither."

The little furball's smile vanishes clean off its face.

The possum coughs and splutters. It heaves and wheezes and hisses. Simon flies from its mouth, into my hands.

"Are you okay?" I whisper.

...*Click.*

I turn to run, cursing myself for falling for that old trick. I mean, I've seen the spell a thousand times. I've seen the Witches' bodies twist and bend and buckle. I've seen their bones snap and crack and pop. I've seen them grow fur and feathers and scales.

So then how could I have fallen for it?

The possum suddenly blocks my way out. Its fur is already shrinking away, and its skin is changing back into robes that are the colour of a dirty and churned-up ocean. Its black beetle eyes are turning bloodshot and sore-looking. Its yellow nails elongate and curl.

Soon, the possum is gone.

And in its place is Scraggleknee.

"Hello, dear," he says, crouched down on the floor and eyeing Simon hungrily. "So, the tasty little morsel is a friend of the Wax Witch, is it? How delightful."

I step back and away from him.

Tuck Simon into my pocket.

Fasten it.

"Scraggleknee did warn Master he should be wary of the Wax Witch." Scraggleknee spits and dribbles as he talks. "Scraggleknee tried to tell him that something troublesome was stirring. That the effigy was not what it seemed. Master wouldn't listen though, would he?" He licks his lips and gnashes his teeth. "But never mind, dear," he says, and grins toothily. "Scraggleknee is perfectly capable of catching you himself."

And then he pounces.

I jump out of the way a fraction too late. Scraggleknee's pointy talons catch me. They slice through wax as easily as knives do butter, leaving three deep scores in my arm.

"ACK!"

It stings like his nails have been steeped in poison. I clutch at the gashes and feel them burning red-hot at their edges, but there's no time to check the damage. I'm already through the door, back out into the night and the protection of the cemetery.

I keep running.

"Don't be like that, dear," the Witch calls out after me. "You're making it so much harder for Scraggleknee to catch you. For Scraggleknee to *destroy* you!"

The sound of his hungry, fleshy snort makes me double down and run faster, even though I know trying to outrun him is pointless. Just like that, Scraggleknee could say a sticking spell or a beckoning charm. Not that he *will* do either of those things.

He'll do something much worse.

Because the three Witches of Elston-Fright have far scarier magics up their sleeves. They've got curses and befuddlements, enchantments and invocations, maledictions and hexes – each one more horrible than the last. More horrible than you can even imagine.

I don't need to look behind me to know that I'm right. Already, witchcraft is pulsing all around me. It ripples through the air and runs over my skin, before it eventually takes hold deep under the earth. It makes the ground shudder and shake. Weeds uproot themselves by my feet. Ants and centipedes flee their homes, scampering away into the night.

"You can't run from Scraggleknee, dear," comes a cackle from behind me. "Because Scraggleknee doesn't need to chase you to catch you."

I glance over my shoulder…

…just as Scraggleknee plunges his hands into the earth.

Things start shaking for real. Huge cracks zigzag their way through the rows of headstones, splitting them in two and sending puffs of stone and dirt and dust into the air. Like an earthquake with the Witch at its centre, the ground fractures at the place where his hands are buried. Cracks branch out and away from him. They swell and shrink as if they're alive. Something beneath the cemetery begins to suck in air from the surface.

Like it's *breathing.*

I jump to the side just as a crack appears right underneath me. I change course. Run in the other direction. But it follows closely behind. It splits into two and comes at me from both sides like pincers. I change directions again but I'm knocked right off my feet. I go somersaulting forwards – "*Wo-OA-argh-*

OH!" – and then land heavily on my face – *THMP!* – where it stinks like damp and rotten soil.

A headstone looms over me.

"Scraggleknee has friends who can help him, dear!" the Witch cries.

The earth stops shaking, and I realize what's about to happen only a second before it does. I don't even have time to scramble to my feet again before a bony hand explodes out of the soil, centimetres in front of my face. I scream. Scurry away from it. Long and scrawny and streaked with dirt, the fist clenches and unclenches.

Like it's reaching for something.

I drag myself away from it just as a second hand emerges and starts groping around. The hand is followed by a skull. Eye sockets come next, packed with soil, and wriggling with glistening worms. Then, a little triangle where a nose would have once been. A single row of teeth – chipped and broken.

And no bottom jaw.

The stench smacks me in the face as Scraggleknee cackles and cheers gleefully. The rest of the skeleton emerges from the grave.

It lets out a wail that cuts right through me.

(Screechy and warbled.)

I jump up. It steps closer.

The skeleton's movement is clumsy and difficult, like it's dragging some huge weight. Its shoulders and back are all hunched over, and its head hangs forward. It reaches out towards me, hands grabbing. I turn to run, and the skeleton chases after me – reluctantly though, like its body doesn't want to. It stumbles and trips. Somewhere, Scraggleknee calls out, "If two feet fail you, friend, why not try four?"

Like a puppet – and the Witch's words the strings – the skeleton's spine starts curving backwards. It's like its wrists are tied up by invisible wires, and Scraggleknee is holding the other ends.

Skeleton hands meet the soil.

With its head dangling backwards from a limp neck, the skeleton begins to scuttle towards me like an upside-down crab. It chases after me again.

Only *much* faster now.

I turn and run –

– but then collide head first into a second skeleton.

There are beetles crawling out from behind its broken spectacles. It takes a swipe at me –

– I jump out of the way.

Its bony hand closes at the spot where I was just standing. The skeleton looks at it, confused, then turns towards me. It takes a single wobbly step in my direction. The first skeleton is coming at me from the other side, now, wailing and warbling and scampering at a furious speed. The second skeleton raises a hand and lunges at me again, but I leap backwards –

– and they crash together. They explode into a mess of bones.

"Never mind," calls Scraggleknee. "There are others."

And he's right. There are *so* many others. On every side of me now, more and more inhabitants of Elston-Fright Cemetery are dragging themselves from their graves and lumbering in my direction. All of them are hunting me.

And *that* gives me an idea.

"Hey!" I shout. "Over here!"

I remind myself that the skeletons are not ghosts like me. They're just zombies, really, if you think about it.

Yanked from their resting places and whipped into a frenzy by evil magic. But no…they are *not* ghosts. And so, what I'm planning to do won't hurt them.

"Come and get me!" I yell.

And then I start running again, as fast as I can.

I duck and dodge their attacks. Leap over and weave between headstones.

Just like I hoped they would, the skeletons follow. They're faster than me, and I know I don't stand a chance at outrunning them, but that's okay. I don't have to outrun them.

Outrunning them isn't part of the plan.

I just need to make it to the cliff edge before they do. Before they get their bony hands on me. "Hold on tight," I whisper to Simon. "You are *not* going to like this."

The cliff is only a handful of strides away now.

Click-click?

Two strides.

CLICK! CLICK?!

One.

CLICK! CLICK-CLICK!

And then I leap right off the edge.

Chapter 15

Help me Fly.

I hope I was right about Elston-Fright Cemetery. I hope its deathly energy really *is* the reason I was able to perform the first Ghostly Act earlier, back when I was Spooking Flip. And I *really* hope that same energy will help me perform the second Act now.

I hope it will help me Fly.

And thankfully…

…it *does.*

Instead of falling into the sea far below, the sky wraps around me like a friend. It catches me and lifts me up, carrying me away from the cliff and out over the ocean.

Wind whips through my seaweed hair.

Cool air rushes over my wax skin.

And then…I stop.

I turn back towards the cliff in time to see the stampede of zombie-skeletons steamroll towards the drop. They're headed straight for it – and they're *not* slowing down.

"Come back, you undead fools!" Scraggleknee cries after them.

The Witch is shuffling behind them, hurrying in the direction of the cliff edge. He is waving his arms about and tripping over his robes, barking orders at his horde of zombie-skeletons. But it's like they don't hear him at all. They're not listening.

They reach the drop. One topples over the edge.

(*They're* not *ghosts*, I remind myself.)

A second follows the first.

Then a third.

More.

The zombie-skeletons pour over the cliff, flailing as they fall towards the rocks waiting down below. Some of them disintegrate like asteroids as they go. Arms and legs and heads come detached until...*Crack! Snap! Crack! Crunch! Snap!*

The noise ricochets off the rock face, echoing all around me, and I have to remind myself one more time that they are *not* ghosts. They're zombies. Still...it's hard not to feel a *little* bit bad for them as they all shatter into skeleton pieces.

The stillness that follows is only broken by the heaving of the ocean way down below. Scraggleknee is peering down at it all.

"Clever trick, Wax Witch," he says to me.

His voice, magically amplified, cuts through the air between us. A crooked but triumphant grin creeps across his face. "Or should I say clever *Act*? Because you're not a Witch at all, are you? Just a pesky poltergeist with a few spells up their sleeve."

His eyes narrow. "Scraggleknee knows *exactly* what to do with ghosts."

I rush forwards.

But I'm too late.

Scraggleknee's arms are raised, and magic is beginning to collect at his fingertips. The air starts to turn all milky. Like a fog, his malediction sweeps across the cliff, forming a wall between me and the cemetery. I try to Fly through it but I can't. The mist flips me upside-down and spits me back out again.

Way above the ocean.

I try again. And then again. But it's hopeless.

As I watch, the strange mist curves over the cemetery, making a sort of half-bubble and sealing the cemetery's deathly energy inside. It breaks the connection between me and the once-ghosts – the ones who lend their abilities to this place. Without the cemetery's help, I can't perform the first or second Ghostly Act. Without the cemetery's help, I can't Fly.

I feel the sky loosen its hold on me. The air jolts.

It quivers.

Shakes.

Scraggleknee is cackling and chortling and coughing now. It comes through the mist all muffled, like my not-ears have been filled with honey. Still, I *just* make out him saying, "Is it true that ghosts can't swim, dear?"

And then, with one last look at the lighthouse…

…I fall.

The lighthouse – with the last Lightkeeper's journals and my only hope of finding the second Spellspring inside it – slip out of sight. I backflip and frontflip, plummeting downwards. Everything becomes a blur. Sky. Water. Rock. Sky. Water. Rock.

I'm seconds away from crashing through the surface.

Any moment now, I'll be eaten up by the waves.

(CLICK!)

But then, far off in the distance…

…I see it.

A fluttering something, darker than the sky around it and streaking through the air towards me. One second, it's just a flicker in the distance. The next –

– it's on top of me.

"Ye-OWCH!" I cry out.

The whatever-it-is has a grip on my seaweed hair and is soaring away from the cemetery, with me in its clutches. My feet dip below the water, kicking up spray as we go. I try to get a better look at the thing that grips me – a giant bat, maybe, or some enormous and hungry bird of prey? – but its outline keeps changing and shifting and morphing. It bends and folds and twists. It swells like a balloon, and then a second later collapses in on itself. It's like it is all of the shapes and none of them, all at the same time.

I reach up, and my hand grazes something smooth and soft and supple. Sort of like waxed canvas or a sailcloth or…or an *oilskin.*

I yank my hand away.

We change direction, shooting straight up. It's a vertical climb, and a moment later we're hovering high above the clifftop. We hang there for a moment. Then, like someone has pulled a carpet out from under us, we fall. We level out and glide over the treetops for a bit before moving lower. Finally – we crash through the canopy.

And I'm dropped on my bum.

"OW!"

The Fisher lands effortlessly in front of me, as if flying is the easiest thing in the entire world. As if they do it all the time and it's no big deal. Except that I know it *is* a big deal. Because even Witches can't fly – at least not without changing into something else first.

Which means the Fisher can't be a fisher after all.

Maybe they were, once.

Before they died.

"Who are you?" I demand, rubbing my head and checking that all of my seaweed hair is still attached. The Fisher doesn't answer. They just reach into their pocket.

"I *know* you can hear me," I say. "I know what you are."

From a pocket, the Fisher extracts a chain – not in their hand, because the Fisher doesn't *have* hands that can hold things. Instead, the cuff of the oilskin's sleeve is all bunched up, with the chain dangling from it. Long and silver, it reflects the moonlight.

And at the end of it is my heart.

"Give that back!" I say. "It's mine."

I don't expect them to actually do it, but they do. The Fisher tosses the heart towards me like it's nothing to them. It soars through the air.

I try to catch it – but I miss.

The heart lands in my lap.

THMP!

I scramble to pick it up and am surprised to find that it's warm to the touch. Hard like silver, somehow the heart still thumps like flesh. Something whooshes at the place where my ears should be – *thmp-thmp-whoosh, thmp-thmp-whoosh* – and when I press two fingers against my wrist, I just about drop the heart in shock. Because, well…

…I have a *pulse.*

"Put it on," the Fisher says.

I'm so distracted by the heart that I don't even register that the voice is a familiar one. I let the heart beat gently in my hands, running my fingers over its grooves and bumps.

Then, I lower the chain over my head.

And the heart grows heavy.

Something warm pours out of it, flooding my not-chest. I ready myself for everything. My name. My memories. The faces of my family. I brace myself for a downpour of answers to my unanswerable questions. They're about to coming rushing back…any moment…

…but they don't.

Nothing happens.

(Something in my not-stomach sinks.)

"Did it work?" the Fisher asks, and this time my head jerks upwards because I *know* that voice. It makes the heart race over my not-chest. "Corpse, did you get your memories?"

I lean forwards, trying to get a look at what's underneath the oilskin hood.

But I can't see anything except shadow.

Thmp-thmp. Thmp-thmp. Thmp-thmp.

The heart beats faster, and the whooshing behind

my not-ears grows too loud to bear. I rip my useless heart off and stuff it into my pocket. "How are you doing that?"

"Doing what?" says the Fisher.

"Speaking in her voice."

The Fisher giggles. "I'm speaking in *my* voice, silly."

"No." I shake my head. "She's gone."

The Fisher throws back the hood of the oilskin to reveal a small face with eyes like topaz. Springy hair, and skin that crackles with little sparks of electricity.

"But...you're dead," I say.

Without responding, she floats off the ground. She starts spinning and twirling in the air. The coat bends this way and that, twisting itself into different shapes. I've seen this happen before. I've seen a ghost Fly, dance and whirl in the air like this. Only last time, that ghost wasn't Spooking an oilskin. She was Spooking a pair of overalls. The ones I'm wearing now.

Girl laughs. "Yeah, I am. But so are you."

Chapter 16

"*I did* just save your death, you know," Girl says, hovering above my head. She keeps up with me without even trying – floating on her back, hands tucked behind her head.

(Honestly, it's like she's *trying* to annoy me.)

I ignore her, and instead focus my energy on stomping through the undergrowth. I want to make sure Girl knows *exactly* how angry I am, so I'm marching along with as much huffing and puffing and crashing as I can manage – head down, arms swinging.

Not that I even know *where* I'm headed, any more.

I should be hurrying back to the lighthouse. I should

be trying to find my way back to Flip and his great-grandad's journals, so I can find out whether the last Lightkeeper knew anything about where the second Spellspring might be. Only, the shock of finding out that Girl didn't vanish into Death Proper after all has got me all confused. The fact that she's been here in Elston-Fright this whole time makes me forget about everything – everything other than stomping and crashing and huffing, that is – and now I have no idea where I am.

Or where I'm going.

"You haven't changed even a tiny bit," Girl says.

She lets herself fall so that she's following behind me, gliding just above the ground and weaving between the tree trunks. Seriously, I have half a mind to…

…actually, no. Not half a mind.

I have a *full* mind to do it.

The very next tree that I pass, I grab hold of one of its biggest and bendiest branches. I drag it forwards and let it spring back at her.

Girl swoops under it with ease.

Urgh.

I try again, hoping that this next one will hit her square in the oilskin – but again, Girl ducks out of the way. Then she zips above my head with a *shwoosh!*

"You know," she says, "a thank you wouldn't hurt."

I stop. Gaze up. Clench my fists.

"A '*thank you*'?" I say. "And what would I be thanking you for, exactly? The part where you left me with the Witches? Or the part where I find out you've been flying around Elston-Fright this whole time, Spooking coats and having a great time? I thought you were gone."

I glare at her. "Girl, I thought you were *dead*."

"I *am* dead. We both are—"

"You know what I mean. Death Proper dead."

Then I turn and keep stomping.

"Corpse, do you even know where you're going?" Girl calls after me.

"Away from you," I reply, without even bothering to look over my shoulder. "And this time, if I'm lucky, maybe I really *won't* have to see you again."

She lands in front of me with a *shwoosh!*

"Take that back."

"No," I say, pleased with the effect my words had on her. "I won't."

I sidestep her, but with another *shwoosh!* she lands in front of me again and throws back her hood. Her skin crackles furiously – like a firecracker.

"You know what?" Girl says. "I take back what I said before. You *have* changed. You've always been a bit selfish, Corpse, and I'm used to that. But now you're *mean*, too."

"Mean?" I shoot back. "*I'm* not the one who said—"

"We *both* said bad things that day," she interrupts, not letting me finish.

But I don't want to talk about that day. I don't want to be reminded of the last conversation Girl and I had before she slipped away into Death Proper. Only…

…well, she didn't slip away into Death Proper, did she?

It turns out she just Flew off to Elston-Fright.

And left me behind.

Girl says, "I didn't wanna leave the rock-that-doesn't-exist, you know. It wasn't my choice. And I *tried* to come back – heaps of times! Only…I couldn't."

What a silly thing to say, I think.

Of course Girl could have come back to the rock-that-doesn't-exist. She can perform the second Ghostly Act, can't she? Unlike me, she can Fly. And since she managed to Fly away from the rock-that-doesn't-exist, there's no reason why she couldn't have flown back to it too. "You could *so* have come back," I tell her. "Whenever you wanted."

"I could *not*. I was banished, Corpse."

(As if that explains anything.)

Girl must realize that I don't have a clue what she's talking about because she sighs. "Let me explain," she says. Her face scrunches up the way it does whenever she's thinking. It's like she's hunting for the right words. Eventually, she says, "The sky around the cemetery – it went all foggy before, didn't it? Scraggleknee did a spell, and it blocked you out of the cemetery? Right before you fell. Right before I *saved* you."

I grit my pebble teeth.

"I wouldn't have needed saving," I remind her, "if you'd just let me take my heart back from the Witches like I was going to, in that alley with the bats. And anyway, why are you asking me that? You know it went all foggy. You saw it yourself."

"No," she says to me. "That's what I'm saying, Corpse. I didn't see it. It only looked that way to you… because Scraggleknee's spell was only *meant* for you."

Then, with a frustrated sigh she adds, "Don't you get it?"

Silence.

Because *no,* I don't get it.

(Not that I'm about to admit that to her.)

"What's this got to do with anything?" I say, annoyed.

Girl groans. "As always, you're not listening to me. I'm trying to tell you that when I look out at the rock-that-doesn't-exist, all I see is this big mist bubble – exactly like the one you saw at the cemetery. I can't Fly through it. It just spits me back out again."

"So…I was *banished* from the cemetery?"

(I've never even heard of a banishment spell.)

Girl nods. "Just like how *I* was banished from the rock-that-doesn't-exist. The Witches got back early that day after our…" – her cheeks crackle pink – "after we *both* said bad stuff." She pauses. "Anyway, I was still out on the tide pools, and I saw them come back. Worst-Witch was all shaky and angry. I snuck closer to try to find out why."

Her face turns kind of sad.

"And?" I push.

"*And,*" she continues, "they were talking about how the rock-that-doesn't-exist's magic had begun to fade. I started running back to the roof to tell you, but Worst-Witch caught me. He said something about ghost vermin. Then he did a spell...and everything went foggy."

And finally...I think I might understand.

"You *couldn't* come back," I realize.

Girl shakes her head. "No."

The truth washes over me like a wave. "*You* sent Old Man to warn me, didn't you? He mentioned someone – someone that he called my *friend*. Was it... was it *you?*"

This time, Girl nods. "It was me."

Half an hour later, we're still trudging through the forest. We've made our way around the back of Elston-Fright, and the ground is beginning to slope upwards. From somewhere overhead, I hear the hooting of a frogmouth – a night-time bird which, even though I can't see it, I know has mottled and tawny feathers. Yellow eyes. A serious face.

Hoot-hoot. Hoot-hoot.

I'm not sure whether Girl and I have stopped fighting or not. I guess the fact that she was banished changes things a bit. And she *did* send Old Man with the warning about my heart, I suppose. But I still feel funny about it all.

Click-click-click.

"Is that right?" Girl coos, in the sugary voice she used to reserve for whenever she was wandering around the rock-that-doesn't-exist's boundary, talking to the water.

She would daydream and dance there.

She would make friends with the critters who lived on the reef.

"*Two-hundred?*" she says now. "That's a lot of

brothers and sisters, Simon. Your parents must have had their hands full. Wait...do spiders have hands?"

And then she giggles.

I make a huffing sound, except nobody hears me. Simon has been sitting on the shoulder of Girl's oilskin for almost the entire time we've been walking, ever since I made the mistake of introducing them. I don't know why it bothers me – but it definitely does.

"Traitor," I mutter quietly.

(*Hoot-hoot-hoot*, goes the frogmouth.)

"Oh," Girl says to Simon, sadly now. "I'm so sorry."

She turns back to me. "Is it true?"

"Is what true?" I ask.

(As if I haven't been listening in the whole time.)

"Simon says that his whole family, that...well, he says that Scraggleknee *ate* them. All of them. And he says that he would have been eaten, too, if you hadn't saved him. He says that after it all happened, you invited him to live in the roof with you."

I don't reply.

"So...is it true?" Girl says.

"Yeah," I say. "So what?"

Girl looks at me strangely. Not in a bad way, exactly. Just in a way that makes me wish she would look somewhere else. "That's a different Corpse to the one I remember."

"And what does *that* mean?"

"The Corpse I know wasn't exactly big on animals. I don't even remember you talking to them, to be honest. Let alone saving them from being eaten."

"I talked to animals all the time."

Girl raises her eyebrows. "Okay, Corpse. If you say so. But you *do* know that talking to animals is different to Po—"

I hold a hand up to stop her. "*Don't* say it."

And then I stare at my feet, feeling something like embarrassed.

"Maybe I've changed," I say. "Did you ever think about that?"

"Honestly? No. But I'm glad to hear it."

Girl's answer annoys me.

Hoot-hoot.

"Where are we going, anyway?" I ask, changing the topic.

Girl has been leading the way. I tried telling her we need to head back the way we came, to the lighthouse, but she said there was no time. She said that we have to hurry. Still...it would be nice if Girl would tell me *where* it is that she's taking me.

"Where are we going?" I try again.

"To get rid of the Witches," Girl says simply.

"Did you...did you say get *rid* of them?"

She nods. "We have to."

I shake my head. "We absolutely do *not* have to."

What is she *talking* about? Why on earth would we go *looking* for Witches? I've spent most of my death trying to get away from them, so I'm not about to seek them out now. Especially not while I've got the treasure that they're after sitting in my pocket.

Not that their so-called treasure seems to do much.

As far as I can tell, my heart is completely useless. Apart from thumping and beating and being all shiny, I don't think it does anything. After everything I went through to find it, I'm no closer to knowing about my family or my name or my memories.

Or finding the second Spellspring, either.

Which makes me wonder…

…why haven't I started to notice my magic fading yet?

I wiggle my pebble teeth, one by one, but none of them budge. I tug at a strand of my seaweed hair, but it doesn't feel like it's coming loose. I even dare to poke myself in the abalone shell eye, but it doesn't move. Nope, as far as I can tell, my magic isn't fading.

Not at all.

"We *do* need to get rid of the Witches," Girl repeats, pulling me back to my senses. "But first, we're gonna need to speak to someone who might know *how* to get rid of them. I know just the person. We'll see if they can help us." She pauses. "Because the Witches won't ever stop searching for your heart, Corpse. They'll never stop searching for *me*, either. Not for as long as they think I've got it. And we can't let them have it. Imagine what they could do—"

"Why not, though?" I interrupt. "It's not like the heart does anything."

Girl stops. Looks at me funny.

Hoot.

"It doesn't do *nothing,*" she says. "I know that maybe it didn't have all of your memories inside it like we thought that it would...but that doesn't mean it does *nothing,* Corpse. And anyway, we probably should have expected that. Because really, when you think about it, I guess it's brains that hold memories, isn't it? Hearts...they hold other things."

"*This* heart holds nothing," I say. "It's completely useless."

She looks at me funny again.

"Corpse, you *do* know that the heart is—"

Snap!

A twig breaking.

"Shh!" I hiss.

I strain to listen, but there's nothing.

It has turned entirely silent again.

Even the frogmouth has stopped hooting.

In my pocket, the heart turns ice-cold. I pull it out to see a fine coating of frost creep across it. At the same time, something turns heavy and cold in my not-chest. "Girl," I begin, "did you understand anything that frogmouth has been hooting about?"

"No," she replies. "I thought that was strange. But then again, I guess it *is* a wild animal, and I don't like telling wild animals what they should or shouldn't do. So, if the frogmouth doesn't feel like talking to us, that's its right. Anyway, what I was trying to tell you is—"

"*Girl,*" I say again. "Listen to me. I think we're being followed."

A voice comes from behind us.

"Massster will be ssso pleasssed," it says, each word oily and slippery like the flick of an eel's tail, "when it isss I who returnsss the locket to him."

From the dark, a figure emerges. The last few downy feathers disappear. In their place, seal fur and cascading midnight hair. Yellow eyes turn purple.

"Ssso very pleasssed."

Chapter 17

"I admit I wasss confusssed at firssst," says Gorflunk, stalking closer, "to sssee the wax effigy and the fisherperssson thief ssstraying through the treesss in sssuch sssilence."

He leers. White teeth flash.

"Then, I undersssstood," he says. "Ghossstsss."

"Put your heart on, Corpse," Girl says to me, and I've never heard her sound so serious. It sounds strange, coming from her. "Trust me. Put it on like you did before."

Gorflunk raises his hands. Magic quivers on the air.

"Do it *NOW*!" Girl shouts.

I don't question what she's telling me to do. There isn't time. I just throw the chain over my head. At the exact same moment, the trees all around us start shuffling forwards like some ancient stick army. They march in unison, creaking and groaning.

Groan. Crick. Groan.

The trees close in on me and Girl, knitting their branches together as they go. With their limbs outstretched, the trees weave themselves together until they've formed a circle.

They wall me and Girl and Simon inside it.

(And Gorflunk, too.)

Cri-i-iiick. Groan.

A branch loops through my elbow from behind. Wraps around my arm. Sharp twigs dig into my wax-flesh like fingers.

I try to pull away, but the tree has me by my other arm as well now. Its grip tightens just as roots explode from the soil and loop around my ankles.

They braid themselves together and pull tight.

Beside me, Girl is all tangled up in tree too.

Gorflunk closes in. "Did you really think that you, two sssad and pathetic ssspectressss, would be a match for the Witchesss of Elssston-Fright?"

"Do it," Girl says to me.

"Do *what*?"

"Witch magic," she says. "Quick!"

Witch magic? There's no chance any spell or charm that I know will make even the tiniest bit of difference right now. I can glue things together and make stuff come to me and turn my fingers into birthday candles. I'm not exactly a match for an army of trees.

"Just trust me," she says urgently.

Overhead, branches have begun to twist and wriggle like snakes.

No...they're more like *eels*.

They pull tight and block out the moonlight, trapping us inside something like a cage. In the growing darkness, Gorflunk's purple eyes glow more brightly.

Twinkling and glittering and cruel.

He steps closer again.

I struggle and strain.

But I can't move.

"Corpse," Girl whispers, and I realize the sound is coming from right by my ear. She's slipped out of the oilskin and is hovering beside me. I find myself wishing I could do the same. But slipping out from an effigy is a bit different to un-Spooking an oilskin coat. I *can't* leave this body now that I've Possessed it. There's only one way to do that, and I promised I would never do it again.

"Do Witch magic," Girl repeats.

"How will that help?"

"Just *do* it!"

Fine.

"Flint and spark will light the dark," I begin, as Gorflunk stalks towards me with his arm outstretched. His fingers clench and unclench. "Birch and fern, they both must burn."

My heart thumps harder against my not-chest.

"For Witches died on the pyre."

My heart turns heavy, and the same warm and powerful something from earlier pours out of it, moving through me. Gorflunk is barely two steps away now.

His fingertips graze the heart.

"Grant me this one wish for fire!" I finish.

Instead of the usual teeny tiny flames appearing at my fingertips, twisting ropes of red-hot fire shoot out from the very centres of my palms. With a blazing flash, Gorflunk is all lit up. Sharp lines. Cutting shadows. He drops to the ground just as my sizzling magic hits the spot where he was standing. It crackles and whooshes. Makes the air around us burn.

Then, just as suddenly –

– it stops.

"How did I do that?" I whisper.

Instead of growing weaker, my magic feels stronger than ever. It hums and thrums beneath my fingertips, begging to be unleashed.

"It's the heart," Girl says. "Now do the other one."

From where Gorflunk is sprawled on the ground, he hisses and splutters. "You disssgusssting, mossst horrible little wax sss—"

"*Do the other one,*" Girl repeats.

"The other what?"

"Magic!" she urges. "The sticking one."

(Oh. Right.)

"Moss on stone and flesh on bone," I start. Immediately, the heart's magic moves through me. I feel myself grow more powerful. "Wings on bat and tail on cat."

Gorflunk is already picking himself up off the ground.

"Like the beak is on a duck."

The heart thumps harder, and my entire body starts to shake and shudder. I'm brimming with so much power now, I worry that I might explode or melt or something.

"Make these two things good and stuck."

SWOOSH!

(That's the sound of Gorflunk falling.)

THWMP!

(And that's him landing back on the ground. Hard.)

"Missserable ghossst. I will tear you apart, limb from wax limb."

Before he gets a chance to say the un-spell, I summon fire again. I know somehow that Girl is right. That the heart is making my magic stronger. That it wants to *help* me. It's like the heart is supercharging my magic or something, making my spells come easily to me.

(*Way* more easily than usual.)

"Go really big this time," says Girl.

(Right. Like I need to be told.)

At my command, ribbons of fire wind up and over my restraints. They burn white-hot this time, but the flames feel like barely more than a tickle against my wax skin.

They reduce the twigs to ash in an instant.

Leaves sizzle. Smoke whips about.

The trees recoil – *crick-crick-swoosh-swoosh* – waving their limbs as they retreat. They twirl and try to put out the fires that are creeping over them.

"We have to get out of here," Girl says.

All around us, trees are uprooting themselves and retreating from my flamethrower hands, leaving gaps big enough to slip through.

"Go!" I urge Girl.

I collect her oilskin from the ground. The trees have let go of it now, and I can hear Simon's *click-click-click*-ing coming from somewhere deep in its folds. I throw it to Girl and watch as she performs Spooking on it, making the oilskin wrap around her.

But then Girl doesn't move.

She just stands there.

Waiting for me.

"I'll follow in a second," I promise. "Go!"

She hesitates, then turns and swoops back out into the open. I face Gorflunk, who has already done the un-spell and is dragging himself from the ground.

"I really do hate ghossstsss," he says to me.

One last time, I bring fire to life. This time, I focus it into a single ball of swirling inferno, right in the palm of my hand. It glows bright, like a tiny sun. Again, it tingles my wax skin, but doesn't burn or melt it. Gorflunk cowers away from it, shielding his face.

I throw the fireball towards his feet and it explodes on impact.

It sets the hem of his seal fur on fire. He screams and stomps and tries to stamp it out. I turn and bolt to the place where Girl and Simon are waiting for me.

"Did you—"

"I didn't hurt him," I tell Girl. "Not really. Now come on!"

Together, the three of us hurry away from Gorflunk and the trees, all of them still trying to extinguish the last of the flames that I magicked. And as we run, away from danger and towards wherever it is that Girl is taking us, an accidental smile creeps over my face. Because *I* just did magic as powerful as any Witch.

Me. A kid ghost.

Chapter 18

Girl and I have stopped fighting. I know it for a fact this time. I guess outsmarting and outrunning a Witch together is the kind of thing that does that. Like a bucket of seawater to the face, it made me forget why I was angry with her in the first place.

"So, the heart is..."

"A Spellspring," Girl finishes. "I thought you knew."

We've stopped at a rocky outcrop while Girl tries to work out which way we need to go from here. She's dropped the oilskin again and is floating just above the treeline, invisible – or at least, invisible to any Witch that might happen to glance this way. To me, she looks like the ghost I remember. Limbs like a bird. Baggy T-shirt. Scrunched shorts.

And skin that crackles faintly in the moonlight.

While she's doing that, I'm sitting on the rock and trying to piece it all together. The heart beats in my hand, but I realize now that it's not beating with memories at all.

It's pulsing with pure magic.

There's nothing more powerful or more terrifying than a kid acting with their whole heart. That's what Old Man said to me, just before he slipped away. At the time, I didn't bother thinking about it too much. To be honest, I kind of thought he was trying to make sure his last words sounded all wise and important. But now that I think about it...

...maybe *this* is what he meant.

"Who was Old Man?" I ask Girl.

She smiles. Lowers herself back to the ground.

"I dunno," she says. "But he was nice, wasn't he?"

I think back to how he appeared out of nowhere, and how I almost jumped out of my wax skin when I turned to find him standing over me. I remember his growly voice.

"He was all right, I guess."

Girl shakes her head. "He was better than all right, Corpse. That was a really nice thing he did, going to warn you." She pauses. "Is he…?"

I nod. "Gone to Death Proper."

Her face drops. "I knew he would. But still…I liked him."

She falls silent but her lips keep moving, and I'm pretty sure she's saying a sort of goodbye to Old Man – which is kind of silly, really, since he's long gone now. Still, I don't say that to her. Girl and I are only *just* back to not fighting, after all.

I don't think calling her silly is a good idea.

Once she's done, Girl Spooks the oilskin again.

It jumps up from the ground and wraps itself around her.

Girl says, "I was trying to find someone like him – someone who could bring you a message – for ages." A darkness crosses her face. "Ever since I followed the Witches to that *disgusting* Ungeneral Store one day.

They were asking about some sort of magic heart."

I run a thumb across my heart, cupped in my palm.

Its magic hums louder. "How did you know it was mine?"

Girl shakes her head. "I just knew. Worst-Witch said they took it from a kid who was snatched thirteen years before. A kid around your age. It all added up."

She sits beside me with a *shwoosh!*

"But the Merchant told him it was gone already," I say, thinking back to what Worst-Witch said to her in the Ungeneral Store. *You told me it had been sold – for a price you couldn't refuse and to someone far away.* "The Merchant lied to him, didn't she?"

Girl nods. "I didn't know she was lying, though. I believed her too."

More pieces fall into place.

"So then you tried to send me a message?" I ask.

"Exactly," Girl says. "The first friend I asked to help was too scared of the Witches, though. I dunno what they did to him, but I reckon it must have been *really* bad. All I know is that he was too frightened to set foot on the rock-that-doesn't-exist again."

"Wait...you made another friend?"

(I don't think I like the idea, exactly.)

Girl isn't listening to me.

A smile has crept its way across her face, nudging aside the darkness that appeared when we started talking about the Merchant and the Witches and the heart-which-is-a-Spellspring. Her face crackles happily. "Then I met Old Man and he was *perfect*."

I'm confused. "But how did he get there?"

Girl looks at me oddly. It's the same look she gave me when I didn't know that my heart was a Spellspring. "What do you mean? How did he get where?"

"To the rock-that-doesn't-exist."

Her brow scrunches up. "He Flew there. Didn't you know he could perform the second Ghostly Act?"

"He didn't mention it," I say drily.

Of course Old Man could Fly. It was the most obvious answer in the world...and I didn't once consider it.

Click-click-click, Simon says from back where he belongs, on my shoulder.

"Yes, Simon," I say. "I realize I probably should have asked him that."

"Anyway," Girl says, "I thought your heart was somewhere far away. I thought the Merchant had sold it. Old Man was supposed to show you that dinghy, then tell you to meet me in the cemetery, so that we could go find it *together*. I waited...but you never came."

I remember how Old Man told me that even though Elston-Fright was dangerous, I wouldn't be alone. "He was trying to tell me, I think. But he slipped away."

Girl nods. "It was while I was in the cemetery waiting for you that I saw the Witches way off in the distance. When I worked out that they were going to the Merchant's house, I knew I had to follow them." She shuffles closer. "I decided to see what they were up to. They magicked their way into her house and broke into her vault. They didn't find what they were looking for, though. Just some old map. Still, they kept on howling about the Merchant being a thief. That's when I knew she still had it. Only, it was too late to tell you by then."

"So then you went to find her yourself," I realize.

"Exactly," Girl says. "I decided to steal it back."

"I saw you. In Elston-Fright."

"You did?"

"Twice," I say. "I thought you were a fisher."

Girl grins. "Then my disguise works perfectly."

She goes on to tell me how she decided to steal the heart herself, then hide it away until the rock-that-doesn't-exist's magic faded completely. She says that once the rock had no magic left in it, she knew it wouldn't be long until the banishment spell broke. "I was gonna Fly across, give your heart back to you, and everything would be better again." Her face lights up with tiny pinpoints of crackling light. "But then I saw you Flying above the cemetery...you came after all!"

And then Girl beams.

I don't point out that I only went to Elston-Fright Cemetery to hide. I don't tell Girl the reason I went there was because I had nowhere else to go.

Instead, I just smile back at her.

I realize now that I've never really thought of Girl as brave or strong. But tonight, listening to everything that she did – everything that she did *for me* – well...

maybe she has changed over the last year. Maybe haunting Elston-Fright has changed her.

Or maybe...maybe she was *always* like this.

Maybe I just didn't see it because she was always daydreaming and dancing and talking to fish. The idea makes me feel strange. I decide to break the awkwardness.

"And then I fell," I say.

Girl giggles. "I Flew faster than I have in my entire death."

Something tugs at the corners of my wax mouth, dragging my smile wider, and I think about what Girl said a moment ago. *I was gonna Fly across, give your heart back to you, and everything would be better again.* But before I get a chance to ask her about it...

...Girl's face turns all serious.

"So *that's* why we've gotta get rid of the Witches," she says. "Because your heart is a Spellspring – and imagine if the Witches had a Spellspring they could take anywhere." Girl shivers. "They could leave Elston-Fright. Snatch kids all over the place."

I know that she's right.

We can't let the Witches do that. With a Spellspring dangling from around Worst-Witch's neck, they could take their snatchings and their curses away from here. They could spread the sickness that hangs over Elston-Fright, far and wide. And besides, I need my heart for myself. I need it for my own magic. And so as wild and as dangerous as her plan is, I do know that Girl is right. We have to get rid of the Witches...before *they* get rid of us.

And now *I* shiver.

We walk in silence for a bit, with Girl up ahead, leading the way.

Something sharp digs into my sides.

It's the shards of the divining bone. I run a hand over them through my overalls and tuck them back into place. I've been thinking about them ever since I used my heart's magic against Gorflunk. Would the second Spellspring make my sticking spell strong enough, I wonder? Could I maybe fix the divining bone after all? Because if I could...wouldn't that mean there's still a chance to find my family? If I could fix the divining bone, I could *ask* it to take me to them.

I decide not to mention this to Girl. Not just yet.

Instead, I say, "You got pretty good at Spooking."

"I've been practising," Girl says happily.

She stops walking for a moment and crouches down to collect a twig from the ground. Her hands are still made of regular ghost nothingness, and so instead it's the oilskin's sleeve that picks it up. The cuff scrunches to form something like a fist, just like it did when she first pulled the heart from the pocket of her oilskin coat.

Girl crushes the twig into pieces that fall to the ground. I step closer to her, then reach out and poke her sleeve with my finger.

The oilskin is all rigid – almost like there's a fleshie under it.

"I got *really* good at it," Girl says.

I decide not to point out how useful this would have been all those times we were trying to find a way off the rock-that-doesn't-exist. I decide not to point out that if she had been this strong at Spooking back then, she could have Flown me over the ocean and across to Elston-Fright – just like she Flew me away from the cemetery earlier tonight.

Nope, I don't say *any* of that.

Still, talking about the Ghostly Acts makes me think about magic, too. And thinking about magic makes me wonder. "Girl," I begin, "if I *had* come and met you in the cemetery – right after Old Man came to warn me about stuff, I mean – and if we *did* go searching for the heart somewhere far away…you know I couldn't have gone very far, right?"

She looks up. "Because of your magic?"

I nod.

"I did think about that. I'm not *totally* silly. But then I remembered that if the rock-that-doesn't-exist is fading…well, it's not like you could stay there either, is it?"

She pauses, like maybe there's more she wants to say.

But also like she doesn't know if she should.

Eventually, she does.

"There's something else, too," she adds. "I reckon

that... Corpse, I reckon that maybe there are other kinds of magic out there. Magic that doesn't come from Spellsprings."

"What do you mean?" I ask.

Girl explains how in the year that she's been haunting Elston-Fright, she's taken to following the Witches whenever they come here. She tells me that there are places in the town that the Witches can't go. Houses that won't let them set foot inside.

Houses that keep them out.

"Any idea what would do that?" Girl asks hopefully.

I think back to the home with the blue kitchen, and how the family inside it seemed to be doing some sort of spell without even meaning to. A spell that was able to keep the Witches' darkness from entering their home. They did it without a Spellspring in sight.

But that doesn't make any sense at all...does it?

"Corpse?" Girl pushes. "Got any idea?"

I shake my head. "None," I say honestly.

But I wish I did.

It's not too much later that Girl announces we can stop walking. She says we've arrived at the place where we'll find the person who can help us get rid of the Witches.

And then she points straight ahead of us.

There, past the last few weedy trees, is a hulking, three-storey manor. Its walls are punctuated with empty windows that don't seem to reflect the moonlight. They look more like holes that you might fall into

– and then never come back out of. The manor sits in the middle of sprawling lawns and a manicured garden that's full of trimmed hedges and a bunch of creepy shrubs cut to look like animals.

"Who lives there?" I ask.

Girl frowns. "You'll see."

We linger at the treeline but don't move. Something about the manor makes me uneasy. Like the Witches' shack and the Ungeneral Store, there's magic in its bones.

We step forwards.

(Or, *I* step forwards. Girl hovers.)

"Stay hidden," I whisper to Simon.

He *click*s in agreement. Moves to my pocket.

Girl and I cross the grass quickly, stopping briefly in the shadow of a shrub shaped like a seahorse skeleton. We pause, look around us, then dart forwards again once we're sure the coast is clear. We stop again, this time beneath a shrub in the shape of a shipwreck. We peer through the darkness. Nothing. Hurry towards a third shrub – a whale, belly up.

Finally, we arrive at the manor's back entrance.

"Can't you just tell me who—"

But Girl presses a finger to her lips, then waves a hand to say I should follow her. Together, we move around the corner to the side of the manor. We pass a window that looks into a grand kitchen, and move past it. A second window reveals a dining room, complete with a big, fancy chandelier. We're just about to pass a third window and turn the corner to the front of the house when Girl's oilskin wraps around my wrist.

She pulls me out of sight.

"There!" Girl hisses. "Look."

I peer through the window and into the darkness. It's hard to make out anything except for another window that overlooks the manor's front. Moonlight pours through it, falling softly on the room's contents. Slowly, shadows inside the room begin to take shape. A grand piano with a sheet draped over it. A bunch of winged armchairs. A fireplace, gaping like a mouth and with a row of silver photo frames – every one of them empty – running along its mantel. Leaning against the far wall is a mirror that reaches almost all the way to the ceiling.

But it's not the mirror that I'm interested in.

It's who is reflected in it.

The nearest armchair is turned away from us, but its reflection in the mirror shows someone is sitting in it. The harder I look, the more she comes into focus. Sitting upright and rigid, the muscles in her neck flex in tiny movements. Clenched fists rest on her lap – tense, and with knuckles white like bone. And stationed all around her…

…a circle of stones and crystals and protective amulets.

I guess the Merchant found a way out of those ropes.

CHAPTER 19

We're standing beside a window that looks into the manor's sitting room.

And together, we're going over our plan.

"I'll do it," Girl says.

It's not like I have much room to argue, given that she's the only one of us who actually *can* do it – without the help of a cemetery, that is. She's the only one who can make her voice heard. The only one who can perform the Ghostly Act of Spooking.

"But do we even *need* a Woeful Ware?" I ask.

"Yes," Girl says matter-of-factly.

I keep thinking back to the Ungeneral Store, and

how close the Merchant came to hurting Simon. And then I think about how I've already lost Girl once. "Are you sure? It's just that I don't think actually *talking* to the Merchant is the best idea. Besides, we've got my heart now, and you *saw* what it can do. Maybe my magic will be enough to get rid of—"

Girl is already shaking her head.

She says, "You know three spells, Corpse. And the Witches have got a whole book full of the things. *Way* worse ones. If they still have malicewater..."

But then, she trails off.

I see her shudder.

And even though she doesn't finish her sentence, I know that Girl is right. If the Witches have their malicewater, they'll still be able to do all their most horrible magics. On the other hand, even though my heart can supercharge my spells, it can't teach me new ones.

So, yes. I do know that Girl is right.

It's just that I *really* don't like it.

I sigh. "Are you sure the Merchant will even want to help us?"

"Of course," Girl says, sounding much surer than I feel. "She *hates* the Witches, Corpse. Especially after tonight. Trust me; she wants them gone as much as we do."

"Fine," I say.

But only because we don't have a better idea.

Then I add, "Be careful, okay? I'll be right here, ready to blast the Merchant with fire" – Girl beams at that bit – "if she tries anything."

Girl promises she'll be back quickly.

She steps towards the window. I try not to think about the last time I saw her, and how she *didn't* come back quickly. She didn't come back *at all*.

The words tumble out of my mouth all at once: "Did you really mean – earlier tonight when you said – did-you-mean-it-when-you-said-you-were-going-to-come-back-to-the-rock-that-doesn't-exist?"

Girl spins around. "What?"

"Did you really mean it?" I say again. "When you said you were going to wait for the banishment spell to break, and then Fly back to the rock-that-doesn't-exist and bring me the heart? Were you *really* going to come back?" I can't meet her eyes. "It's just...we were always talking about getting away from there. Were you really going to come *back*?"

At that, Girl actually giggles.

She pulls a face. "Did you think I was gonna stay in Elston-Fright for the rest of my death or something? I've been trying to get back to the rock-that-doesn't-exist ever since that first day I was banished." She pauses, and then she smiles. "I'm your *friend*, Corpse."

The place where my tummy should be fills with warmth.

Girl turns on her heel.

And the oilskin lands in a pile on the ground.

She walks through the sitting room wall like it's made of smoke, and then emerges on the other side of it looking like herself again. Skinny arms and legs. Bare feet. She's invisible to the Merchant, obviously. But then, as I watch, she performs the first Ghostly Act. She Spooks the sheet on the grand piano, making it lift into the air and settle over her ghostly frame.

I nudge the window ajar. Simon scuttles off my shoulder.

He moves to the windowsill so he can hear what's going on inside.

Girl approaches the Merchant from behind. She reaches the back of the armchair.

And then she starts Spooking the Merchant, too.

"Boo!"

The Merchant is out of her chair in a flash. She spins around…

…then her shoulders slump.

"A *ghost*?" she says with a scowl.

Girl starts Flying, making the sheet billow around her. She rises towards the ceiling – twisting and twirling like a dress dancing under water – and then she glides over the top of the Merchant's head. Finally, she lowers herself into the armchair opposite.

"That's right," Girl says sweetly. "A ghost."

The Merchant doesn't let her scowl drop.

"Well," she says, "I suppose the Witches think they are very clever, sending somebody dead." Even from here, I can see that her eyes keep darting around her, like the Witches could be anywhere. "I guess that makes *these*" – she gestures at the circle of protective talismans – "completely and utterly useless." She kicks angrily at one of the crystals.

It bounces.

Shatters.

The Merchant shakes her head and says, "Imagine sending a ghost to do your dirty work. Those Witches will stoop to anything. *Nothing* is below them."

"That's not it," Girl says.

My whole wax body feels tense, like it's turned to stone. And it's as if a piece of coral has lodged itself in the throat that I don't even have. Girl, on the other hand…

…is just sitting there, looking cool as a sea cucumber.

Has she always been like this?

(Brave, I mean.)

"Do you really expect me to believe they are not here?" the Merchant says to Girl with a bite. She strides to the window – the front window, that is, not the one I'm hiding outside – and squints to see outside. "Where are they?" she snaps. "Where is *he*?"

"I told you, I've got nothing to do with the Witches."

But then Girl pauses. "Well…not *nothing*."

"See?" says the Merchant. "I knew it. Where are—"

"—they *did* snatch me," Girl interrupts. "Ages ago."

The Merchant falls silent. Something passes behind her eyes. They narrow. I can almost hear her brain whirring from here. She stares out the window a moment more, but then seems to make up her mind about something. The Merchant turns around to face Girl.

"Did they now?" she says. "How horrible."

In three long strides, the Merchant is back at her armchair. She sits down and considers Girl for a while, like she's trying to work out whether or not to trust her. She must decide to, though, because she says, "Those Witches have wronged me too, you know."

"I *do* know," Girl replies. "That's why I'm here."

The Merchant shakes her head. "I am not sure I follow."

"You and me," Girl says, "we have a…what do they call them? A common enemy?" She thinks on it for a second. "Yeah, that's it! A common enemy."

The Merchant nods. "I suppose we do."

"Well, I'm gonna get rid of them."

The Merchant gives Girl a weird look and barks a mean little laugh. "*You*?" she says. "A child ghost, hidden beneath a sheet, against the three Witches of Elston-Fright?"

Beneath her cover, Girl shakes her head.

The fabric twists this way and that.

"First of all," Girl says, "it's not very nice to make fun of people for what they choose to wear. And I can *so* get rid of the Witches. I'm not doing it on my own."

The Merchant raises her eyebrows. "O*h*?"

"Me and my friend Corpse are gonna get rid of the Witches together," Girl says. "She's a ghost too. Only, we need your help. We need one of your Woeful Wares."

Maybe I'm imagining it…

…but it seems like the corners of the Merchant's lips twitch.

"And which Ware might that be, child?" she asks.

"Whichever one can get rid of Witches."

Ten minutes later and Girl has explained the whole thing.

The Merchant reacted in all the right places. She scowled when Girl told her about the Witches' wonky shack, and then she actually gasped out loud when Girl revealed that it's tucked inside a secret rock that fleshies don't even know about – that fleshies *can't* even know about. "That explains it!" said the Merchant. "And how would one go about getting to this rock, exactly? And the book they call *Magikal Maledictions*… it is there?"

Girl paused. "Why do you care about their book?"

The Merchant waved the question away.

"It is not important," she said.

Girl seemed to accept the Merchant's response without question, but it got me thinking: why *does* she care about their book so much? If the Witches were right about that map of hers, and if she really *has* been hunting them, then *why*?

What use is *Magikal Maledictions* to her?

I didn't get long to question it, though, because pretty soon after that the topic of conversation turned to me. Girl didn't tell the Merchant everything, obviously. That would be dangerous. She just told her that we haunted the roof of the Witches' shack together, and that I'm her friend. She didn't tell the Merchant that I have the heart, and she *definitely* didn't tell her that I'm crouched outside the sitting room window right this second.

"So," Girl says now, "where's that Woeful Ware?"

"I think I might have *just* the thing," the Merchant says, stroking her chin with a finger and staring into space through narrowed eyes. "I keep a handful of my most precious Wares here in the house – for personal use, you understand. But before we get into all that, I first want to make sure that you understand how dangerous what you're suggesting is."

"I do," says Girl automatically.

The Merchant smiles – but it's a strange smile that doesn't quite reach her eyes. "Well, you *are* brave," she says. "And what exactly will you do after you" – she gestures something going *POOF!* with her hands – "eradicate the vermin?"

Girl shrugs beneath the sheet. "I guess Corpse and

I will go back to haunting their shack with our friend Simon. He's a huntsman spider...and he's *very* wonderful."

I run a hand over the divining bone pieces and feel guilty.

But Girl will understand. Finding our homes and our families is what we said we were going to do, wasn't it? That was *always* our plan. And so, she'll understand that I still want to find them. That I want to repair the bone with my heart's magic and go looking for them.

We can do it together. She'll want that too...

...won't she?

"How *lovely*," the Merchant says to Girl. "It sounds to me like you have got it all sorted out. And this... Corpse, did you say her name was?" Girl nods. "Well, she is a lucky ghost to have a friend like you. But remind me, because I am an older lady than I appear and so forget these things, how long did you say Corpse has been haunting that shack?"

"Oh," Girl replies airily, "I didn't. Ages, I guess. She doesn't really remember. All she knows is that after the Witches snatched her, they stole her heart and—"

Girl stops.

But it's too late. She already let the truth slip.

The Merchant runs a hand over her neck, down to the place where up until only hours ago the heart had sat. Her nostrils flare, and the little muscles in her jaw clench. Without meaning to, my own hand squeezes tightly around the locket – around *my* heart – and I feel it start to thump nervously. *Girl*, I think to myself. *What have you done?*

Quickly, I drop the heart, raise my hands…

…and ready myself to do magic.

Chapter 20

I don't actually *do* magic though. Not yet.

With my hands raised and power buzzing about my fingertips, I wait.

"What I-I meant was..." Girl stutters.

But the Merchant is smiling at Girl. She shakes her head, then presses a finger to her lips. Gently, she says, "Do not worry, child. Your secret is safe with me."

Wait, what?

It is?

"As you say," the Merchant continues, "the Witches are our common enemy. Now, wait here. I will go and collect the Ware that will set things right."

Then she gets up.

And she leaves the sitting room.

I can see the air wriggling by my fingertips. I can feel the palms of my hands tickle. My whole body is humming with magic, expecting a spell. But still… I wait.

Because we need that Woeful Ware.

And it looks like the Merchant is actually going to give it to us, too.

When the Merchant returns a few moments later, it's with something small cradled in her hands. Whatever it is, it's hidden beneath a covering made of the same sapphire velvet as the curtain in her Ungeneral Store. "Here it is," she says. "Your Woeful Ware."

Girl floats out of her seat and glides closer to take a look.

The Merchant twists away. "Uh-uh-uh," she says. "Not just yet. I still need to explain how to work it." She sits down, rests the Woeful Ware on her lap and strokes it like a cat. "But first, how about you tell me more about this friend of yours? This…*Corpse*, was it?"

Girl sits back down. "Yeah. But why do you wanna know about her?"

"No reason," the Merchant says airily. "Just being polite."

It's not very convincing, though – not at all.

(Why *does* she want to know about me?)

"I don't believe you," Girl says warily.

"All right, *fine*," the Merchant replies. "I will admit I am a little curious about your friend. Because...well, I suppose you could say she is a friend of mine, too."

"What does *that* mean?" I say to Simon.

Click, he replies – as confused as I am.

"Friends don't wear friends' organs as jewellery," Girl points out.

A shadow crosses the Merchant's face, and I'm sure that Girl's words have angered her. I decide that enough is enough. It's time to get Girl out of there. We'll take the Woeful Ware and run. We can work out how to use it ourselves – *without* the Merchant.

And so, I start to do a spell.

I mutter the magic words. Straight away, twisting threads of fire spring to life. They snake their way across my hands. But just then the Merchant's eyes narrow, her grin turns sharp, and she says to Girl, "I have known your friend longer than you have, child."

My spell fizzles out. The magic dissolves into nothing.

Around my neck, my heart starts beating harder.

"Simon!" I hiss. "Did she just say—"

Click-click!

"What does that mean…she's *known* me?"

Click-click-click.

"You…*know* Corpse?" Girl asks the Merchant, confused.

The Merchant shakes her head and waggles a finger.

"You need to listen more closely. I said I have *known* her. Although, perhaps it would be more accurate to say that I *knew* her." She pauses. "I knew her when she was alive."

My heart *really* starts thumping now.

"*What?*" I hiss.

Beneath the sheet, Girl twists her head in my direction. The Merchant notices and turns towards the window as well. I duck out of the way – just in time.

"Where is she?" the Merchant says, squinting. "Is she here?"

"No!" Girl says quickly. "*No*. Corpse is… somewhere else."

It's a terrible lie, and I'm pretty sure there's no way that the Merchant is actually going to believe her. But I guess I'm wrong because the Merchant doesn't question it. And a few moments later, after Simon lets me know that the coast is clear, I peer back through the window to find that the Merchant has already turned back around to face Girl.

"You left her alone?" she asks.

"She's with Simon," Girl replies.

The Merchant pauses for a moment, like she's thinking it over. "Funny," she says, "you do not strike me as the kind of ghost who would leave a friend behind."

Click-click-click-click, Simon says to me.

And I agree. Something feels…*off*.

I bring my magic to life again.

But for some reason I still don't do a spell.

"Did you *really* know Corpse?" Girl asks doubtfully.

My magic sputters and dies.

I drop my hands.

It's because I need to hear the Merchant's answer, I realize. That's why I can't bring myself to do a spell. This is the closest I've come to getting answers to my questions. It's like I can sense them, right there on the tip of the Merchant's tongue, waiting to be spoken. The air has turned heavy with unsaid things. And so...

...I need to hear just a *little* bit more.

I lean closer to the gap under the window and try to block out the whooshing and thumping that has sprung to life behind my not-ears. I open the window a little further.

"Better than anyone," the Merchant says.

"Better than her friends?" Girl asks doubtfully.

The Merchant scoffs. "She had none of those."

"Better than her *family*, then?"

At that, the Merchant laughs out loud.

"Corpse had no family," she says.

The entire night turns still around me. The heart, which until now had been beating hard and fast, stops beating altogether. The thumping and the whooshing sound fades, leaving behind a hollow and ringing silence. Something in my not-chest aches, and when I look down at the heart locket, I notice a tiny bruise has appeared in its very centre. As I watch…

…the bruise spreads outwards.

"Your friend was not from Elston-Fright," the Merchant tells Girl. "She was simply dumped here one day, a long time ago and by travellers who saw this forgotten town as the perfect opportunity to… unburden themselves. Nobody knows who they were, so there is no point in asking me about any of that. All that is known of them is that they left a car here, with a crying baby in its back seat, and that then they fled as quickly as they arrived."

"Didn't anybody help her?" Girl says.

The Merchant appears to think on it for a bit.

"In a manner of speaking," she replies. "Corpse was taken in – if that is what you mean. She found a home to grow up in. She turned into a horrible child, though."

"She did not!"

The Merchant leans forward. "Of course she did. Have you seen what happens to a child when they live a life without love? There is no hunger quite like loneliness. They become *starved*. Hunched shoulders. Empty eyes – eyes that eventually turn mean."

"Corpse *isn't* mean."

The Merchant raises an eyebrow. "Is that so?" she says, smirking. "Then Corpse has never teased you? The two of you have never had a fight?" She leans closer to Girl and in a quieter voice, says, "Be honest… has she *always* been such a great friend to you?"

Girl pauses.

My not-stomach sinks.

"As I suspected," says the Merchant.

(And she sits back in her armchair, satisfied.)

"Well," Girl says, and there's an edge in her voice now, "if Corpse *does* do mean things sometimes, it's only because mean things were done to her first. It sounds to me like Corpse was just a good person who spent far too much time being treated badly by horrible people. Anyway, you're wrong. Corpse does *so* have friends. She has me. *And* she has Simon."

But the Merchant waves her words away. "Corpse was a horrible child that nobody loved," she says. "I of all people should know that…given that I raised her."

The heart frosts over.

My chest burns like ice.

It's like Girl has forgotten how to speak. She sits in silence for a time, before voicing exactly what it is I'm thinking, "Wait…*you're* the one who took her in?"

The Merchant nods.

"You mean Corpse lived *here*?"

"For twelve years," replies the Merchant. "I was the one who found her, back on that day when she was left behind by her so-called *family*. I brought her to live here."

"Then you must know what her real name is!"

The Merchant looks confused. "I am quite sure that I never gave her one."

"No *name*?" Girl says. "No name in twelve whole years? No name in the entire time she lived here? No name at all before…before she was snatched by the Witches?"

At that, the Merchant laughs.

"Snatched by Witches?" she repeats. "Do not be ridiculous, child. I have never heard anything so absurd.

The Witches cannot even set foot inside the houses of Elston-Fright. How would they snatch a child?" She adjusts herself in her chair. "No…that is not what happened."

The Merchant's words make me think about the house with the little blue kitchen, and how it was protected from the dark magic that surrounded it, left behind by the Witches. Her words make me think about what Girl said earlier, about how there are places in Elston-Fright where the Witches can't go. Still, I don't understand. I *have* to have been snatched.

"What happened, then?" Girl pushes.

"Are you sure you want to know?" the Merchant asks.

"Yes. I'm sure."

(*This is it*, I think.)

The Merchant nods. "Very well."

She fidgets with the covering over the Woeful Ware. "As I am sure you can appreciate, one meets all sorts in my line of work. My magical oddities; they attract buyers from every shadowy pocket of the globe. They bring rumours with them. Stories of ancient magics and forgotten rituals." Her eyes twinkle. "I heard one such rumour. A means to preserve magic in silver. I waited a very long time for the right child to arrive, then one day she appeared almost as if by some delicious destiny. I found her, abandoned and alone in that car."

Simon starts clicking at me from the windowsill.

"Shhhh," I tell him. "Not now."

CLICK-CLICK! he says urgently.

"Shush, Simon."

CLICK!

I cup a hand over him. "Shush!"

(I *have* to hear this.)

The Merchant smiles a crooked smile. "But I needed her to grow up first. And I needed a Witch to perform the ritual. Greedy fools, they had no idea what they were agreeing to. They did not question the instructions I gave them when I handed your friend over. With a tear in my eye, I asked only that they return her heart to me, bound in silver. They did not know they were crafting me a Spellspring." Her smile twists into something terrible. It looks like she has more teeth than is normal. "I suppose what I am telling you is that your friend was never snatched by Witches because the only person who does any snatchings around here is *me*."

The heart freezes solid.

It was *her*.

"I traded your friend with the Witches," the Merchant says. "As I do with all of the children I snatch. But this was different. Her heart was part of our deal, fair and square."

CLICK-CLICK-CLICK!

Simon escapes from under my hand and jumps up and down on the window frame. He jabs a leg in the direction of the manor's front gate. Striding towards the manor is a figure – impossibly tall and frail, like a teetering tower of ash. The figure has shadowy eye sockets with something like embers buried deep in their depths.

I spin back towards the sitting room window.

"Girl, get out!" I shout. "Get out now!"

But she doesn't hear me. "Fair and square?" she says. The sheet goes flying off and I can see her again, angry sparks crackling to life around clenched fists. She levitates up and out of the armchair. "None of that is *fair and square*." She flies higher. "None of it!"

"Girl!" I shout. "Worst-Witch is here!"

She *still* doesn't hear me.

"NONE OF THAT IS FAIR AND SQUARE!" she yells.

The Merchant whips the cover from the Woeful Ware.

At first, I think it's a normal bottle – long, and shaped like a triangle. But then I remember being crammed inside that cupboard at the Ungeneral Store. There was a whole shelf lined with things just like it. The tag attached had read: *BANSHEE-IN-A-BOTTLE*.

Then, in smaller print: *for trapping ghosts*.

"GIRL, RUN!"

Chapter 21

"GET OUT! GET OUT! GET OUT!" I keep yelling.

But Girl doesn't hear me –

– until finally she does.

I jam the window open, and she turns and rockets towards it. With my hands pointed squarely at the Merchant behind her, I start my spell. The Merchant doesn't even notice me. She just unstoppers the bottle and starts laughing wildly.

The heart comes back to life. It beats and pulses and grows heavy, pouring its magic into me. My fingertips prickle with the promise of fire. But then I stumble over the magic words when Girl runs head first into some invisible barrier with a *THUMP!*

She drops straight to the floor.

"I have caught you, ghostie," says the Merchant. "*Fair and square.*"

Girl's eyes – wide and fearful – meet mine.

"You are not going anywhere," the Merchant taunts through a hungry grin. "I know that was your little friend Corpse in my Ungeneral Store tonight. I *know* it. And I know she is somewhere here on my grounds. When she comes for you...she *will* lead me to the place where the Witches hide. She will take me to where the locket is. And the *book.*"

And finally, I understand.

The Merchant wants *Magikal Maledictions* for the same reason she wants my heart. She wants a book of spells as much as she wants a Spellspring.

Because if she has both of them...

...she can become a *Witch.*

Girl squeaks when her feet begin to liquefy.

(Or gas-ify. Or melt. Or...*something.*)

She starts to be pulled backwards, towards the open

banshee-in-a-bottle. Everything below her knees becomes a blur. Like water being sucked down a plughole, it swirls and whirls and twists. As I watch, the rest of her starts to do the same.

At the same time, runes start to appear across the banshee-in-a-bottle, catching what little light falls through the window. Faint at first, they grow clearer as more of Girl is sucked into the bottle. I know straight away that, even though the Merchant can't see Girl now she's stopped Spooking the sheet, the runes tell her that the banshee-in-a-bottle is working.

I hurry to start my spell: "Flint and spark will light the dark."

"GO!" Girl yells at me.

"Birch and fern, they both must burn," I continue, picturing a blaze more terrifying than anything I've ever magicked before. "For Witches died on the pyre."

Two enormous fireballs come alive.

They churn angrily in my palms.

"Grant me this one wish for—"

But then a slick voice by my ear breaks my concentration.

"There you are, ssslippery little ssspectre."

And Gorflunk rips the heart locket from around my neck.

I fall backwards. Land roughly on the grass.

The fireballs vanish to nothing.

"Girl!" I shout.

A second figure grabs me by the shoulders.

"Did you think you could outrun us, dear?" it says.

Scraggleknee drags me to my feet, his nails cutting into me.

I elbow him in the guts. Push him away and aim a kick right at his kneecaps. He crumples to the floor with a shriek. Gorflunk cackles with laughter.

"Brought to your kneesss by a ghossst," he teases.

Gorflunk moves to lower the locket over his head, but I lunge at him, and he comes tumbling down, too. He lets go of the heart locket and it lands not far away. I leap towards it, snatch it up and move to put it on. As I risk a glance through the sitting room window – only Girl's head, neck and shoulders are left, not yet been swallowed up by the banshee-in-a-bottle – Scraggleknee grabs me by the ankles. I fall to the ground.

Someone snatches the heart from my grip.

And a second later –

SQUELCH!

– I'm hit by a sticking spell. Except *this* time, instead of sticking my feet to the ground, the magic binds my legs together at the knees, like they're glued together.

SQUELCH!

Then, at the ankles too.

SQUELCH! SQUELCH!

Both my arms are pinned to my side.

SQUELCH! SQUELCH! SQUELCH!

Sticking spell after sticking spell strikes my wax body, binding it together. I roll around on the ground, but I can't get back up. I can't see through the window, either.

I don't know what's happened to Girl.

"We've got you now, dear," crows Scraggleknee.

Gorflunk has me by my right arm, Scraggleknee by my left.

And looking down at me is Worst-Witch.

"Welcome back," he wheezes. "For a being made of wax and sea rubbish, you have an infuriating knack for getting in our way...*ghost*." Up close, his breath stinks. "Yes, you bothersome little brat, Scraggleknee and Gorflunk have informed me of what you are."

The other Witches chuckle and guffaw.

I try to pull away from them but can't.

My whole body is still stuck together with sticking spells.

We're out the front of the Merchant's manor. Worst-Witch sneers at me, then reaches into his pocket and pulls out a tiny vial of something crimson like blood, half emptied already.

Malicewater.

He takes a sip of it and his eyes glow red. He turns on his heel, marches towards the door and knocks three times. Then Worst-Witch waits. And waits some more.

Eventually, I hear a shuffling sound from inside.

The door opens, but only a little bit. Enough for a single hand to be poked through it – a hand that is gripping one of the protective amulets that was on the sitting room floor. Almost perfectly round, the amulet is covered in shallow craters. It's the size of an orange but the colour of stardust, and with a milky halo that turns more solid in the moonlight.

Through the crack between the door and its frame, I can barely make out the whites of the Merchant's eyes.

She says, "So, you did come after all. To what do I owe the dishonour this time?"

Worst-Witch doesn't answer her.

Instead, he waves a hand towards the door, and it swings wide open. Fuelled with a fresh dose of malicewater, his magic is powerful. The door crashes into the wall behind it. Then, with a second wave of Worst-Witch's hand, the Merchant comes flying through the doorway.

She lands roughly on the ground with an "OOPH!"

Worst-Witch raises his hands again. With a *BANG!* the door to the Merchant's manor slams shut behind her. Then with a *SQUELCH!* it is sealed up tight.

The Merchant scrambles to her feet.

She hurries back and away from the Witches, her eyes flitting from one to the next. Her once-sharp hair is ruffled from the fall, and her crisp suit hangs off her shoulder. Her free hand darts to her pocket, checking the banshee-in-a-bottle that is poking out from it.

"It has become clear," says Worst-Witch, "that your treachery knows no limits, Merchant." He starts stalking around her. "I came here on the suspicion that you might have been liaising with the ghost thieves tonight." He points to me, and then to something by Gorflunk's ankles – Girl's oilskin. "And I see now that my suspicions were correct."

He shakes his head. "Pitiful company. Even for you."

That's when the Merchant finally notices me, tucked between Gorflunk and Scraggleknee. Her eyes widen when she sees me. Her hand races to her pocket again, to check the banshee-in-a-bottle. Her other hand tightens around the amulet-orb-thing.

"Simon," I hiss. "Simon, where are you?"

From somewhere to my left, I hear a *click-click-click*. He's tucked deep inside Scraggleknee's robes, I realize – probably pocketed with a plan to eat him later.

"I'll get you out," I whisper. "I promise."

(Only…I have no idea *how* I'll do it.)

"I am afraid I am going to have to ask you to leave my property," the Merchant says, pointing the amulet directly at Worst-Witch like a weapon. "You are not welcome here."

Gorflunk laughs. "We do not ssseek your welcome."

"Go," the Merchant orders. "Now."

(But her voice shakes.)

"Scraggleknee," Worst-Witch says, extending a bony hand at him. "The locket, if you will. I'd like to show the Merchant how it's *supposed* to be used."

The Merchant points the amulet at Scraggleknee.

"Do *not* move," she says.

Scraggleknee chuckles as he shuffles towards Worst-Witch, extracting the heart locket from his pocket as he goes. If he's worried about the amulet, he doesn't show it.

He hands my heart to Worst-Witch.

"Stop!" the Merchant says. "You are mistaken. I have no interest in ghosts."

As the Merchant speaks, something invisible –

something like an idea – passes behind her eyes. But the Witches don't even seem to notice. The Merchant reaches for her pocket and extracts the banshee-in-a-bottle. She holds it out for Worst-Witch to take. Something where my stomach should be twists and aches because inside the Woeful Ware, swirling and crackling and sparking like a storm trapped in a teacup, is Girl.

The Merchant says, "The ghosts are no allies of mine."

She holds the banshee-in-a-bottle cupped in her hand, waiting for Worst-Witch to take it. "I caught this one," she says. "I intended it to be a gift to you."

I see her swallow. Hair sticks to her temples.

"A sort of peace offering," she says.

Worst-Witch stalks forward and snatches the banshee-in-a-bottle from her. He holds it up to his eye, inspecting the runes. "And who exactly do we have trapped inside this?"

The Merchant steadies herself.

"I have trapped the ghost of the girl whose heart you are wearing," she lies. "As you no doubt remember,

I raised her, and so I suppose she must still haunt this place." She takes a deep breath. "Whatever the reason, tonight she made herself known to me and I discovered that she means you harm." There's the tiniest of shakes in the Merchant's voice when she adds, "So please, just take her. But leave the ghost made of wax in return."

"Why would I do that?" Worst-Witch rasps.

"I have…an *academic* interest in it."

Worst-Witch stalks closer to her.

"*Liar,*" he wheezes.

The Merchant flinches.

Gorflunk and Scraggleknee chuckle and snort.

"You toyed with fate when you lied to us about the whereabouts of the locket," Worst-Witch says to the Merchant, tucking the banshee-in-a-bottle into his belt. He lowers my heart over his head, and straight away I feel its magic respond to him. A darkness gravitates towards Worst-Witch, buzzing around his fingertips and waiting for him to shape it into a spell.

"And you *sealed* it by lying to me again now," he continues.

The Merchant aims the amulet at him, but Worst-

Witch waves his arm through the air and the amulet shoots into the sky like a comet. It explodes like a firework.

Pieces rain down around us.

"Did you really think a moonstone could protect you?" says Worst-Witch, amused. "How quaint. Its light cannot touch us – cannot *find* us – shrouded in darkness as we are."

The veiling tonic, I think.

"Your services will no longer be required by us," Worst-Witch says to the Merchant. "And your time as a trader of the world's finest Woeful Wares has come to an end."

He starts a spell.

Two white clouds swarm like bees around Worst-Witch's hands. Deep in his empty sockets, a flash of blood red. Somewhere in the air, a humming sound.

The Merchant falls to her knees.

"Spare me," she says. "Please, I did not mean to—"

Worst-Witch sneers. "Who is *really* in this banshee-in-a-bottle?"

The Merchant's eyes flit towards me.

Her face is shiny now. Her eyes are wide like coins.

"You don't have much time," Worst-Witch warns her.

(The buzzing around his hands grows more intense.)

"All right!" says the Merchant. She points at me. "*That* is the ghost whose heart was turned into the Spellspring. The ghost in the bottle is her friend. They are on my grounds tonight because it is *they* who conspire against you. Not me. They are working together to rid Elston-Fright of Witches. I assure you this is the whole truth. Now please…spare me."

For a moment, nobody says a thing.

There's only the sound of magic buzzing.

The Merchant trembles. "*Please.*"

Worst-Witch leans down until his face is almost touching hers. She shivers and shakes. "I will never forget the sound of you begging," Worst-Witch says.

Then he releases the swarms.

"NO!" The Merchant springs from the ground.

And she runs.

She bolts down the path and towards the manor's front gate, the clouds buzzing after her. But she barely makes it a few strides before Worst-Witch calls out after her:

"You cannot run from the Witches of Elston-Fright."

The Merchant is halfway to the gate when the swarms catch her. She screams out – "PLEASE, YOUR WICKEDNESS!" – as they merge around her to form one big cloud. It wraps around her, shrouding her completely. And the buzzing grows louder.

"PLEASE…STOP THIS!"

The buzzing gets louder and louder.

Soon it's loud enough to muffle her cries.

The noise becomes unbearable until – just like that – it stops. Everything turns quiet, and the cloud dissolves into the air like it was never there. Once the magic clears, the Merchant has vanished. All that remains where she stood is a sculpture made of ice.

No…not ice.

Sea glass, polished smooth and the colour of aquamarine.

It gleams faintly in the moonlight. A statue of the Merchant, mouth open in a scream, frozen in time and cursed to spend forever running from the Witches.

Chapter 22

The Witches are still cackling and cheering long after they've marched through the gate and away from the Merchant's manor, deep into the surrounding forest. I'm dangling over Scraggleknee's shoulder, from where everything looks topsy-turvy and upside-down. All around us, trees loom high. They throw mean and flickering shadows.

And from somewhere close by comes the sound of rushing water.

(Water, which I know might be my only chance to escape.)

"A ssstroke of geniusss, Massster!" says Gorflunk

happily. "Not that I would expect anything lesss from a power of your magnitude."

"While I quite agree that my curse on the Merchant was a magnificent display of magic, Gorflunk," Worst-Witch rasps, "you might be more effective at locating vessels for our journey back to the rock with that ceaselessly yabbering mouth of yours *shut*."

Scraggleknee scoffs. "Another stroke of genius, Sir."

"You too, Scraggleknee," says Worst-Witch.

Scraggleknee digs his nails deeper into my ankles – out of annoyance, I guess. But I refuse to let the pain show. I can't draw attention to myself.

Or else he'll notice that I've come unstuck.

Un-spelling the Witches' sticking spells took longer than it would have done if I was still wearing my heart. Without it, my magics have shrunk back to the way they were before. They're *smaller* again. Still, I guess I'm lucky to be able to do them at all. I worried that without the heart to draw from, I wouldn't have *any* magic left. But somehow…

…I still do.

I don't know whether it's lingering from my time wearing the heart locket, or if it's traces of magic left from the rock-that-doesn't-exist. Or maybe it's neither of those things. Maybe Girl was right when she said, *I reckon that maybe there are other kinds of magic out there. Magic that doesn't come from Spellsprings.*

Whatever the reason, it turns out I still had enough magic to undo the Witches' sticking spells. But because they did so *many* sticking spells on me, I had to say the un-spell over and over again. Each time, a little more of the Witches' magic came undone.

With my first un-spell, I was able to wriggle my fingertips.

My toes were next. Then elbows and wrists.

Eventually, I was able to undo the whole thing. Now, I'm riffling carefully through the deep and smelly folds of Scraggleknee's robes, trying to find Simon.

"I'm coming," I tell him.

From some hidden pocket, I hear him *click*.

"I'll find you."

Click-click, he says.

"Hold on. I'm coming, I promise."

I twist my head around to make sure the other Witches aren't watching and am relieved to see that neither have noticed me. Gorflunk is a few strides ahead of us, and Worst-Witch is at the front of the group. I feel sick when I see Girl in the bottle tucked into his belt.

"And then I'm coming for you next," I whisper.

The Witches step onto a wooden footbridge, and down below I hear rushing water. The creek underneath us sounds like it's freshly fed by the storm, and running fast.

This is my chance. I have to hurry.

My fingers brush leather.

It wriggles.

Click-click!

I pull a little drawstring bag from Scraggleknee's robes. Inside it, I can feel Simon kicking and squirming. I hold it close to my not-chest.

"You're okay!" I tell him.

Click-click-click.

We're halfway across the bridge now, and I know this will be my only shot. The flowing water will move us away from this place quickly. It will be dangerous – and I have no idea where it will take us – but it's not like outrunning the Witches is an option.

Yes, I tell myself. *This is the only way.*

I clench my teeth, tense everything and then jam my elbows into the fleshy bit under Scraggleknee's ribs with every bit of oomph left in my little wax body.

He gives a muffled cry. Keels over.

I drop heavily to the ground.

And then I spring quickly to my feet.

"The wax ghost!" he cries. "Get her!"

I've already pelted away from him, though.

Soon, I pass Gorflunk too.

The banshee-in-a-bottle is swinging from Worst-Witch's belt and is almost close enough for me to grab. Two more steps. Now, one more step. My arm is outstretched towards it. My fingertips graze the glass. Worst-Witch spins around.

"You *little*—"

But he's too late.

I've already ripped the banshee-in-a-bottle from him and am striding away from the Witches – with

Girl safely in my hands. I leap up onto the rail that runs the length of the bridge and am about to jump when someone grabs me and snatches Simon from my grip.

"That morsel belongs to Scraggleknee!"

"Give her to me!" yells Worst-Witch, shouldering Scraggleknee aside and grabbing me by the front of my overalls. I try to push him away, but he's stronger than he looks.

He pulls Girl easily from my hand.

I struggle. Kick and punch. But it does nothing. Worst-Witch's teeth are grey and cracked and horrible. His tongue, a blackened stump. And his breath is like dead mice and vinegar. Something pearly collects at the corners of his lips. "Is it true?" he rasps. "What the Merchant said?" He lifts the banshee-in-a-bottle. "Is this a *friend* of yours?"

The heels of my feet find the back of the railing and I nearly topple over. Far below, the water thunders and crashes. Worst-Witch shakes me.

"IS IT TRUE?" he shouts.

Reluctantly, fearfully…

…I nod.

"Good," he purrs, so softly now that I doubt the other Witches can even hear him. He presses his face so close to mine, I want to scream. "Then it will give me no end of pleasure when I dispose of them." He grins. "There is a malediction for this very purpose, you know. A powerful magic to send spectral annoyances to their second death."

I reach out for Girl, but he pulls her away. I struggle against his hold, but he grips me tighter. I make a grab for the heart, but I miss.

He pushes me closer to the edge.

"I've never performed the magic," Worst-Witch continues, "but I cannot think of a better use for my new Spellspring than to deliver your friend to Death Proper." His ember-like eyes bore into my abalone-shell ones. "Not you, though. Tonight, your troubles have earned you a more terrible kind of torture." He leers. "Say goodbye, little ghost, because your friend will be gone by sunrise. And enjoy the rest of your death, knowing that they are no more."

Then he lets go of me. And I fall.

I cry out. My arms and legs flail about.

But nobody comes to rescue me this time.

The banshee-in-a-bottle, with Girl crackling fiercely inside it, grows smaller and smaller. The Witches' faces become harder to make out. And by the time I crash into the water, they're just dark silhouettes cutting against the night sky.

Ker-SPLOOSH!

I bob to the surface, only for a second, before I'm dragged under again. The current releases me and I float – but not for long. Soon, I'm back under water. I thrash and twist and tumble. Crash into rocks, hidden beneath the surface. I smash against the creek's bank, then get sucked back into its flow. I'm moving further and further from the bridge.

From Girl. And Simon.

I float for a moment before being swept under again. This time, I don't come back up. The current sucks me down. Holds me there.

And it doesn't let me go.

By the time I float back to the surface, I should have died ten times over.

(If I was a fleshie, that is.)

I rise from the muddy creek bed into an estuary, calm and sandy. I don't even realize I'm floating towards the edge because I gave up fighting any current a while ago. I bump into the bank, and it takes me a while to remember that I should probably do something about it.

I drag myself from the water. Crawl forwards…

…and collapse.

The bank feels cold and wet against the back of my neck and arms. My entire wax body stings, criss-crossed with cuts and nicks and scratches. But none of that compares to the feeling that comes each time I think about what Worst-Witch said to me before dropping me off the bridge. I look up to the sky and see that the night has reached its darkest.

Say goodbye, little ghost, because your friend will be gone by sunrise.

Enjoy the rest of your death, knowing that they are no more.

The darkest part of the night always comes just before the morning, and so I know that sunrise will be here soon. And when it arrives, Girl will be gone.

For good, this time.

Simon, too. Simon who came with me tonight, even though he's a spider and spiders are supposed to be scared of everything. They'll both be gone. They both *are* gone.

And it's because of me.

I should never have let Girl Spook the Merchant in the first place. I knew it was dangerous. And when she did, I should have got her out of there sooner. We should have run far away from that manor. Instead, I stayed there because I wanted to hear what the Merchant knew. Because I wanted *answers*. And so, because of me...

...the Merchant trapped Girl.

And Scraggleknee took Simon.

It's all my fault, just like it was all my fault that she was out on the tide pools alone on *that* day. It was my fault nobody was with her when Worst-Witch caught her.

When he *banished* her.

Here on the bank of the estuary, my abalone shell eyes start to prickle and sting like they did in the cemetery. This time, though, I don't try to stop it. This time, I let a single trickle escape from one of them. It rolls down over my cheek...and drops away.

But then another comes. And another.

More and more.

Soon there are two little streams pouring down the sides of my face. I sit up. Rest my head between my knees. I wrap my arms around them and pull them in tight. I feel myself choke on the growing sadness. It washes through me and pours out.

Little salty raindrops fall away from me, landing on the sand.

Drip. Drip. Drip.

An invisible weight presses down on me from all sides and wraps me up. At the same time, it's like my insides are being hollowed out. An ache grows in my not-chest.

"I'm so sorry," I whisper.

Chapter 23

It was a normal day, just like any other, really.

The sun was high in the sky, and its blistering heat made the rock-that-doesn't-exist stink like the dried seaweed that was piled up around its edges – putrid, but somehow kind of familiar and friendly, too. The Witches were away doing horrible Witch stuff, and so Girl and I had taken to exploring the tide pools like we always did when they were away.

Except…Girl had gone and wandered off, hadn't she?

The last time I saw her, she had been asking each of the clouds whether or not they'd had a nice morning – and so, for obvious reasons, I decided to leave her to it.

Only now I couldn't find her *anywhere*.

"Girl!" I called out. "Where are you?"

I scampered over the tide pools trying to find her.

Until, finally, I heard her voice.

"Corpse! Hey, Corpse!"

I spun around to find Girl Flying towards me at top speed, with wide eyes and an even wider smile. Crackling with excitement, she landed. "You'll never guess what I found!"

"Whatever it is can wait," I told her. "I need to show you something."

She beamed. "No, *I* need to show *you* something. Come on."

But whatever it was that Girl wanted me to see so badly, now was *not* the time. What I had to show her was more important. While Girl had been off doing whatever it was that she had been doing, I had managed to pull off something that would change *everything*. I had found what we had been looking for – for two whole years. And besides, knowing Girl, the thing she wanted to show me was probably just a funny-shaped barnacle.

Or maybe a particularly friendly herring.

"Later," I said. "Follow me."

"But Corpse, I found something! I found—"

"*Later,*" I repeated. "This is important."

Girl seemed like she was about to argue.

But she didn't.

Instead, she sighed. "Fine. Your thing first...*then* mine."

I led Girl around the rock-that-doesn't-exist, moving more slowly than I would have liked because every few minutes, Girl's overalls came un-Spooked and she would have to re-Spook them all over again. Soon, we arrived at the side of the rock-that-doesn't-exist that gets the most sun. Drenched in light that day, the whole thing was alive with wriggling geckos. Smooth, scaly and with tails like whips, they darted in and out of the cracks, soaking up the day's heat and only ducking away to hide when a hungry gull would fly too close.

"Oooh, hello cuties!" Girl greeted them cheerily.

I snapped my fingers right in front of her face.

"Hey!" I said. "Earth to Girl. Listen up."

She looked up at me and frowned.

"That's not very nice," she said.

I just ignored her.

"I need you to pay attention," I said, my body fizzing with excitement now. I'd been working on my plan in secret for weeks, whenever Girl wandered off, but that morning was the first time I'd actually managed to pull it off. I *really* hoped that I would be able to do it again. "I've worked out how I'll do it," I said. "I've worked out how I can get off the rock-that-doesn't-exist so that we can go get our answers in the town-that-nobody-visits."

"That's what I'm trying to tell you! I found a—"

I held up a hand. "My thing first," I reminded her.

Again, Girl seemed like she was about to argue. She glanced over her shoulder, towards her favourite spot – the place where the rock-that-doesn't-exist folds in on itself, with its rising-and-falling waters and its giant mounds of weed and sand.

Then, Girl glanced back at me and sighed.

"*Fine*," she grumbled.

Something about the way she said it annoyed me,

but I chose to ignore that for now. Instead, I turned to face the rock-that-doesn't-exist and its hundreds of geckos. "I can't Fly like you," I said, "so it's not like I can just zip over the water and start looking for my family, right? And I can't Spook, so even if we did find them, I couldn't talk to them anyway."

"Oka-a-ay," Girl said. "But we already knew that."

I did my beckoning charm, and a tiny gecko whizzed into my hand. I placed it on a little rocky ledge, and when it tried to scurry away into a crack, I magicked it in place with a sticking spell. All four of its feet became glued to the rock. It couldn't move. Not at all.

"What are you doing?" Girl said. "Stop that!"

I shook my head. "Shush, please. Remember how I always said that if I left this body, I would probably slip away into Death Proper? Remember?"

Girl gave me an uncertain sort of nod.

"Well," I said proudly, "I found a way around that little problem."

"Corpse," Girl said slowly. "Un-spell the gecko now, please."

She was staring at me funny. Suspicious. Worried.

Again, I shook my head. "It's *fine*, Girl."

"But you're scaring him!"

"Can you please stop worrying about lizards and start listening to me, instead? You know, your *actual* friend? I'm trying to tell you that I know how I can leave this wax body. I've been practising. Living things are harder to Possess than effigies, but—"

"What?!" Girl interrupted. "*Living* things?"

Her eyes flitted from me to the gecko.

"Just…watch this," I said.

Then I crouched down so that I was staring directly into the gecko's beady eyes, and I pictured what life must look like through them. I imagined days spent sunning myself and hiding from giant seagulls. And as I did it, I felt an invisible connection spring to life – a sort of corridor between me and the gecko, who had turned all still and glassy-eyed. "I *can* leave this wax body," I explained to Girl, "but only if I head straight into another one."

"Stop!" Girl shouted.

And then she darted between me and the gecko.

Her overalls blocked the critter from view. Straight

away I felt the connection that had been growing between me and it break. "I won't let you do that, Corpse," Girl said. "I won't let you use the third Ghostly Act on him. You can't Possess an innocent little lizard."

She shook her head at me. "It's…it's just wrong."

"*Wrong*?!"

Being told off by Girl embarrassed me. The way she was talking to me made me feel suddenly silly. And being made to feel embarrassed and silly…

…well, that made me *angry*.

I laughed at her. "And *let* me? Who made you the boss?"

"Nobody is the boss in a friendship, Corpse."

I thought then that Girl looked every bit as angry as I was feeling. Furious sparks had started crackling over her skin, and her fists were clenched. "Possessing something alive is horrible," she said. "Why would you do that?"

I stood up tall.

"Oh, I don't know," I said sarcastically, my voice rising. "Maybe so that I can get off this old rock?

So that I can find my family, like we *said* we would?"

"As...as a *lizard*?" Girl asked doubtfully.

I wish I hadn't said what I did next, but I couldn't help it.

The words just bubbled up inside of me.

And then...they exploded outwards.

"As a kid!" I yelled at her.

In the long moments that followed, the only sounds were the lapping of the waves and a lazy squawking from somewhere overhead. Girl stepped back and away from me, shaking her head. She was staring at me like she'd never seen me properly before now.

"I'm only *practising* on the geckos," I said angrily, "until I'm good enough to Possess something bigger. Something like a shark or a dolphin or a pelican. Something that can swim or fly to the other side. Then, once I get to the town-that-nobody-visits..."

I trailed off. My face turned warm.

Out loud, my plan sounded horrible.

Girl said, "Corpse, building an effigy to Possess is one thing. But doing the Ghostly Act on an actual fleshie kid? That would make you as bad as the Witches."

The words struck me like a tidal wave.

"Don't follow me," I growled. I turned and marched away from her, heading back around the rock-that-doesn't-exist – towards the cave and the shack. I heard Girl call out for me to come back, but I didn't reply. I just kept on stomping away from her.

I wanted to get away from her and back to my roof.

"Corpse, come back. Corpse, *wait up*!"

She zipped over my head and landed in front of me. "Listen to me. You *can't* use Possession like that, and I reckon you know it already. There's more though…"

She trailed off and shook her head.

"Actually, no," she said. "Don't worry about it."

"What?" I sneered. "Go on."

Girl sighed, like maybe she was readying herself to say something that had been on her mind for ages. She didn't look angry any more. More kind of sad. "Corpse," she said. "I know that finding our families and our names is important, but it's just that…well, I've been thinking. You *do* know that even after we find them… well, you know that we can't go back to being fleshies, right? You know that you'll still be you, right? A ghost."

She paused. Then, she said, "Some things can't be undone."

"What would you know?" I growled at her.

"You're not the only one who was snatched, Corpse."

"Maybe not. But I'm the only one who seems to care."

Girl shook her head. "I *do* care."

"Then start acting like it!" I shouted. "You run around this rock like it's the best place in the world. It's like…it's almost like you actually enjoy being dead or something."

I remember scowling at her, then. "Don't you *want* to find your family?"

Girl fell silent. Her cheeks crackled faintly pink.

Eventually, she said, "You know that sometimes things don't look the way you think they will, right? Sometimes *family* doesn't look the way you think it will."

The pink sparkles on her face grew brighter.

And the colour in them grew deeper.

Girl stared at her feet.

"We do have each other, you know," she said. "So, it's not like we don't have *any* family." She looked back up at me. "Don't you reckon?"

I don't know why I said what I did next. Maybe I wanted to hurt her, the way she had hurt me when she said I was as bad as the Witches. I don't know. All I remember is that I took aim with my words and said, "No, Girl. I don't *reckon*. You're *not* my family."

Girl recoiled like she'd been stung by a poisonous jellyfish.

Her face fell. The little sparkles went out.

I pulled my face into a scowl. "You barely even act like my friend any more," I said. Then, for good measure, "You're just some ghost who turned up in my roof one day."

Girl didn't say anything for a moment.

And when she did, her voice trembled. "When did you become so *mean*?"

I told Girl not to bother coming back to my roof, and I stormed away. I left her behind me, and it wasn't until hours later that I finally calmed down enough to realize what I'd done. Hours later that I regretted everything I'd said. And after all the anger seeped away…

…I just felt kind of sick.

The Witches had returned by the time I stepped outside to try to find her. It was dark out and I searched the tide pools for ages. I hunted everywhere, calling Girl's name over and over, but there was no sign of her. The very last place I checked was the part of the rock-that-doesn't-exist that folds in on itself, because I remembered that's where Girl had been trying to show me something earlier that day. I thought perhaps she was hiding there to teach me a lesson. But I didn't get past the entry to the chasm sort-of-thing because that was where I stumbled across it – a fabric something, floating sadly in the water.

Her overalls.

At first, it felt as if I'd turned all hollow. Or like the world had been pulled from under my feet. Like I had died all over again…because it had finally happened.

Girl had been taken by Death Proper.

She was gone.

After that day, I promised myself I would never

Possess another living thing. I swore that I would never use the third Ghostly Act again. And as time passed and months moved by, I got used to the fact I would probably never leave the rock-that-doesn't-exist.

"Sorry," I whisper again now. "Girl, I'm so sorry. And Simon."

My eyes are still leaking.

"You're both gone. And it's all my fault."

I rock back and forth, talking to nobody on the bank of the silty, slimy estuary.

Or at least...I *thought* I was talking to nobody.

But it turns out somebody *does* hear me.

Ahead, the estuary begins to bubble and ripple and churn. I look up in time to see waves rolling across its surface. Something under water is moving towards me.

Chapter 24

"You again?" I say, scampering back and away from the lumbering silhouette rising from the water. Because even though they *did* let me and Simon go earlier, I'm still not one hundred per cent sure whether the monster made of kelp is a friend or an enemy.

"What do you want?" I ask.

The monster is shaped like a person again, not an octopus – a person made of knotted weed and long spines, with needle teeth that glisten in the moonlight. Their silver eyes are wide, and they're waving their hands about like they're trying to convince me that they aren't going to hurt me. I sort of believe them, too. But then I think about how I ignored the bad feelings I had about the Merchant earlier.

And look how that turned out.

The monster staggers forward and drops to their slimy knees. They scratch something into the silt. I can barely see it though, so I quickly mutter the words of my fire hex. Just like when I reversed the Witches' sticking spells and escaped Scraggleknee, I'm relieved to find my spell works. A little flame appears at my fingertip. I still have magic in me.

Good.

I step a little closer and extend my hand towards the patch of sand where the kelp monster has written two short words. In the flickering light, I can just make them out.

NEED HALP?

"You want to halp – I mean, *help* me?"

The monster nods so furiously that water rains down all over me.

"But…why? I don't get it. You don't even know me."

They lean down again to write something new.

GURLFREND

I nearly choke. "I am *not* your girlfriend!"

The monster shakes their head and hastily crosses out that last message.

~~*GURLFREND*~~

They replace it with two separate words:

GURL FREND

The monster jabs one long and spindly finger at the first word, then points to themself. Finally, they point at the second word.

When I don't get it, they do it all over again.

And then one more time.

"Oh!" I say, jumping up. Suddenly, it all makes sense. "Girl told me she made a friend here in Elston-Fright." I remember she said that before meeting Old Man, she asked some other friend to come and deliver me the warning about my heart. "That friend is you, isn't it?"

The monster nods happily, then points at the word *GURL* again. This time, they point at me afterwards. Then at the word *FREND*. Then back at me again.

Lastly, the monster shrugs.

"Yes," I tell them. "Girl is my friend, too. And so is Simon. Do you remember him? The spider. Wait...do you know what a spider is?"

The monster nods.

"It's too late, though," I say. "They're gone. The Witches took them."

The monster shakes their head at me again, then points to the sky. At first, I struggle to make out what they're trying to show me. But then I see it. Out to sea and in the distance are the silhouettes of three birds. Cormorants, if I had to guess. It's hard to tell from here.

As we watch, the birds fly swiftly towards the rock-that-doesn't-exist. When they near it, the air around the rock starts to wobble. It's like there's some invisible bubble over the top of it, and they've just broken through it. A shockwave ripples through the air.

Milky and foggy and white.

I'm certain that by taking Girl back there, the Witches have broken their own banishment spell on her. Whether or not they know they did it is another story. Either way, the Witches sink lower in the sky and vanish into the rock-that-doesn't-exist's shadow before they land.

"How would we even get out there?" I ask the monster. "I'm not sure how much you monsters know about us ghosts, but we can't swim. Not even a little bit."

The monster just blinks at me.

"What?"

They circle the words *NEED HALP*?

"You can help me get there? To their shack? But… Girl told me…she told me that you're scared of the Witches."

One last time, they point at the word *FREND*.

"You'll do it because she's your friend?"

The monster nods. Smiles a smile that is ugly and full of kindness.

I sense the hint of a pulse spring to life. It's strange

because it *almost* feels as if I'm wearing the heart locket all over again. But that can't be right, because the heart is far away, back on the rock-that-doesn't-exist, hanging around Worst-Witch's neck. Still...

...I can *definitely* feel magic stirring inside me.

The phantom pulse grows stronger.

I don't know where it's coming from, but the only way I can make any sense of it is to believe that Girl was right when she said there is some sort of magic that doesn't come from Spellsprings. I still don't know exactly *what* that magic is, only that it seems to grow stronger whenever I think about Girl and Simon. When I do, the pulsing feeling moves to some place deep in my not-chest, where it collects and starts *thump-thump-thump*ing.

Then it spreads down my arms and all the way to my fingers.

It moves down to my toes, too, until all of me begins to hum, just like I did all those years ago when I found the little black button discarded in the tide pools. Whatever this feeling is – whatever this *magic* is – I know it doesn't belong to my wax body. It belongs to some invisible part of me that I don't know the name of. Whatever the magic is, the family who live in the house with the blue kitchen had lots of it. And now, it seems that I've got it too.

Or maybe…maybe I've *always* had it.

But didn't know it until tonight.

I nod to the monster.

"Let's go."

It's a wild ride getting back to the rock-that-doesn't-exist.

The monster moves faster than I could have imagined, rocketing along the seabed in their octopus shape, with me clinging on for dear death. We corkscrew the entire way, terrifying the wrasse and whiting and stingrays that find themselves in our path.

And in no time at all, we're back where I started.

The monster and I stride across the tide pools, creep through the cave and come to a stop outside the Witches' shack. From the outside, its rusted walls sit at strange angles, propped up on rotting beams. If possible, it looks even more shabby than when I left it.

"Remember the plan," I whisper to the monster.

They nod back at me. Glance nervously over their shoulder.

"Girl. Simon. Heart." I check each one off my fingers as I go. "We need to free Girl from the banshee-in-a-bottle, take Simon back from Scraggleknee and then get my heart back so that Worst-Witch can't do any more magic with it. That last part's important."

(*Just not as important as getting Girl and Simon back*, I think.)

I tiptoe towards the shack's only window.

It's thick and yellow and covered in cracks.

"Stay here," I instruct the monster. "I'll distract the Witches. They won't expect you, and so wait until I give you the signal—"

The monster nods. They already know the rest.

The window distorts and twists what's inside the shack, but I can still make out the familiar parts that I know so well. The hundred flickering candles. The book stand that holds *Magikal Maledictions*. The concoction bench. "Wait right here," I say to the monster.

And I sneak towards the front door.

I nudge it open just a tiny bit. Enough so that I can get a clearer view without being seen. The Witches are gathered in the room's centre. Worst-Witch has my heart around his neck, and all three of them are gazing down at the fire pit. Instead of a fire, though, the pit has been filled with dark water. Scraggleknee begins to stalk around it, an empty vial in his hand. Its glass is slick with something red. Scraggleknee starts muttering to himself, magicking the water to swirl like a whirlpool. It sinks at its centre and twists like a cyclone.

And hanging above it, suspended on a string…

…is Girl.

The banshee-in-a-bottle spins on some glistening thread. Like all of the Merchant's Woeful Wares, it's too heavy with magic, so beckoning it isn't an option.

We'll have to stick to the plan and take it by force.

Scraggleknee stops pacing. "It is ready, Master," he announces.

"Well done, Scraggleknee," replies Worst-Witch.

Gorflunk scowls. "A sssatisssfactory job."

Scraggleknee glares back at him and sneers.

"The good book says that a porthole into death can only be opened by the most gifted of sorcerers," continues Worst-Witch. He's standing behind the book stand now, reading from *Magikal Maledictions*. "Which means that by definition, the responsibility will fall to me."

My heart is around his neck. He caresses it between a thumb and forefinger.

Something angry bubbles up inside me at the sight.

And without meaning to, I clench my fists.

"Scraggleknee, you will keep the waters moving," Worst-Witch drawls, reciting instructions from the page. "And I will open the passage between here and Death Proper. Is it within your abilities, Gorflunk, to cast the Woeful Ware into it?"

"Of coursssе, Masssster. I would be hon—"

But Worst-Witch holds up a hand.

"Then let us begin," he says.

Scraggleknee raises his hands in the air, closes his eyes and continues to enchant the waters. They swirl harder and faster than before, sloshing up and over the edge. The fire pit starts to make a churning, gurgling, rushing sound. It's like the whirlpool is taking in air to feed itself. Like it's *alive.* The edges of Scraggleknee's robes flutter on the air, drawn to it. Gorflunk moves to the pit, unties the banshee-in-a-bottle and cradles it in his hands.

Then Worst-Witch begins his magic.

In the centre of the swirling waters, a single point of bright light appears. It starts to grow larger, until I find that I can't look directly at it. Something like voices echo out of it, and it takes me a moment to realize that I'm listening to the rumblings of a billion dead souls.

I feel myself shrink away from the shack's door.

(Away from the porthole into Death Proper.)

"Drop it in now," Worst-Witch orders Gorflunk, who is still holding the banshee-in-a-bottle. A single ghostly arm reaches up and out of the whirlpool. The groaning grows louder. "Quickly," Worst-Witch snaps, "before the dead start climbing back out of the thing."

I turn back to the monster.

"Wait for my signal," I remind them.

Then I crash through the door with a *BANG!*

Gorflunk's head whips in my direction.

"Ghossst!" he hisses.

I launch forwards, bowling him over. The banshee-in-a-bottle goes flying out of his hand, and I crash into the far wall. The bottle soars. Eyes flooded with the fear, Gorflunk catches it – but only just. He lands on the floor, rolls over and inspects the bottle for cracks. Then, he takes aim at me.

"You pesssky little—"

I dodge the bolt of lightning he sends in my direction and leap towards the book stand. I reach for the heart around Worst-Witch's neck, but he takes a swipe at me –

"You again! HOW?!"

– and I have to duck away.

I manage to grab *Magikal Maledictions*. I slam it

shut and tuck it under my arm. Then, I race across the room and leap up onto the concoction bench.

(Dodging another of Gorflunk's lightning bolts as I go.)

Without the book, Worst-Witch doesn't know the words to his spell, so straight away the porthole into Death Proper begins to shrink. "Do *not* stop your spell!" he orders Scraggleknee. "Continue the malediction. Keep the waters moving. I will take care of this."

Scraggleknee's eyes are closed in concentration.

And so, I take my chance.

"Out of luck and out of reach," I say, hands outstretched. "You I need, you I beseech. Thing I seek, please come hither. Hurry now, don't you dither."

The drawstring bag with Simon inside it flies out of his pocket and rushes into my hand just as Worst-Witch sends two jets of fire in my direction – not from the palms of his hands, but from the depths of his fiery eye sockets. I smell something like singed seaweed.

But I've already leaped away.

Both blasts of fire miss me, instead leaving two smoking holes right in the spot I was standing only a second ago. "Dispose of the ghost," orders Worst-Witch. I realize that he's not talking about me – he's talking about Girl. Gorflunk moves to the whirlpool, arm outstretched.

"NOW!" I yell.

The monster bursts into the shack. They snatch the banshee-in-a-bottle from Gorflunk's grip and with a single kick send the Witch flying across the room.

Gorflunk crashes into the wall.

He crumples on the floor.

"YES!" I cheer, punching at the air.

The monster collects Scraggleknee. Lifts him high overhead. With a piercing cry, they throw Scraggleknee on top of Gorflunk. Both Witches go limp, and I cheer again…

…just as Worst-Witch's magic strikes me in the chest.

CHAPTER 25

A scorching pain smacks my chest. I drop to the floor and roll.

The fire goes out.

My hand rushes to the charred hole it left in my overalls to find that the wax underneath it has turned all gooey. It drips around its edges like thick and sticky blood.

"Ah, the neighbourhood *weresquid,*" says Worst-Witch. He's turned on the kelp monster now. His wheezing, rattling voice is dripping with distaste. "It's been so many years since we last saw each other. Tell me, was my wrath not enough for you the first time?"

And then he shoots a spell at the monster.

(Who I guess is a weresquid.)

The monster dodges Worst-Witch's attacks. Their kelp un-weaves and re-weaves itself into new and strange shapes. Every time a blast of fire is sent their way, the weresquid changes into a different form so that it whizzes right past them.

The weresquid throws their fair share of punches, too.

Beyond where Worst-Witch and the weresquid are locked in battle, Scraggleknee and Gorflunk are beginning to wake up.

Gorflunk tries and fails to push Scraggleknee up and away from him – "Get *off* me, you oaf!" – while Scraggleknee groans and moans but doesn't budge.

Click!

Simon, who has slipped out of the drawstring bag, is jumping up and down beside *Magikal Maledictions*, which fell open on the floor when I dropped it.

"Are you sure?" I ask him.

Click-click.

"But it will be dangerous."

Click-click-click.

"Okay," I say. "If you're sure."

I begin to flick through the book's pages, stopping only when a pained *SKWEEE-oargh!* makes the whole shack shake. The weresquid is floating off the ground, electrified. They've taken a hit from Gorflunk, who sent a lightning bolt at them from down on the floor.

Scraggleknee and Gorflunk scramble to their feet.

I tear my eyes from them and keep hunting through *Magikal Maledictions*. There are whole chapters on "Glamours and Guises", "Bemusements and Befuddlements", and "Revenges and Retributions". I flick past them and – "Here it is!" – find the spell we're looking for.

"I've never tried this before," I warn Simon. "What if it doesn't work?"

CLICK! he says. *CLICK! CLICK!*

"Fine," I say. "Here goes nothing."

THE ELEPHANTINE ENCHANTMENT*

From small like a flea, or wee as a gnat;

To tall like a tiger, the fearsome cat.

The top of your head, the tip of your toe;
From crown to tail, I command you to grow.

Incantation Notation: ↑ ← ↑ →

*Strictly for use on members of the classes mammalia, reptilia, aves and insecta. Use on other members of the animal kingdom, and in particular on arachnida, may lead to dastardly results and, if performed, is at the Witch's own peril.

I speak the spell, being careful to follow the notation perfectly. I make sure I get my rhythm just right, directing my hands upwards and leftwards and rightwards in the way the book tells me to. I'll only get one shot at this, and I can't afford to mess it up.

But when I finish the enchantment, nothing happens.

...click?

"I don't know," I say. "I must have done something wrong—"

CLICK!

The sound explodes out of Simon as his entire body balloons outwards. In an instant, he grows to the size of a labrador, except with eight glassy black eyes arranged in two rows. He has giant pincers and a coating of thick and matted grey-brown hair.

I fall backwards. "Whooooa..."

Simon doesn't wait around. He springs straight past me and collides with Scraggleknee – who had been charging at us – in mid-air. Simon tackles him to the ground, then rushes to start folding Scraggleknee's robes over the top of each other. His back legs become a blur as he knits Scraggleknee into a sort of cocoon. And when he's done, the Witch has become all wrapped up like a mummy. Simon drags him into the next room.

Gorflunk chases after them.

SKWEEE-oargh!

I look up to find both the weresquid's arms are on fire. Their kelp is burning to ash and falling away, while plumes of white smoke pour out of Worst-Witch's eye sockets. The weresquid throws the banshee-in-a-bottle towards me and I catch it – but only just.

Then, and with one last sorry glance in my direction…

…the weresquid barrels forward.

They crash out of the door.

The weresquid wails all the way back to the safety of the ocean – *SKWEEE-oargh!* – until, from somewhere in the distance, I hear an almighty *SPLASH!*

Worst-Witch has already turned back to me.

"Miserable brat!" he says.

And quick as a flash, he does a spell.

Before I can do anything, I'm lifted off the floor and sent rocketing backwards, dropping the bottle. I collide with the wall behind me and fall to the concoction bench.

Worst-Witch utters a second spell, and a rope shoots at me from some corner I can't see. Just like it did with Merchant in the Ungeneral Store earlier, the rope wraps around me over and over. It ties me to the concoction bench. I struggle and strain, but I'm stuck. Out of the corner of my eye, I see the banshee-in-a-bottle glow more furiously where I dropped it. It shakes and rolls along the floor, and I know Girl is trying to escape and help me.

Worst-Witch strides forward and snatches it up.

Then he collects *Magikal Maledictions*.

"That's enough magic from you," he says.

He turns towards the pit of swirling water, the banshee-in-a-bottle in one hand, the spell book in the other and my heart around his neck. I struggle and strain against my bindings, but I can't move. I can't do *anything*, except watch on helplessly as Worst-Witch holds Girl out over the porthole into Death Proper. The bright white light is still shrinking.

"Simon!" I call out. "Simon, help!"

But he doesn't reply. The next room has fallen completely silent. No struggling from Scraggleknee.

No hissing from Gorflunk. And no clicking from Simon.

"Say goodbye to your friend," sneers Worst-Witch.

The white light grows smaller.

CLICK-CLICK-CLICK!

Simon thunders back into the room. He springs forward, crossing the room with ease, but Worst-Witch steps back just in time and so Simon misses him. Instead, the spider's outstretched leg accidentally loops through the chain around Worst-Witch's neck.

The clasp breaks. The locket drops to the floor.

No – not the floor.

Towards the pit.

"My locket!" Worst-Witch shouts. He grabs at it but misses. Fumbles and stumbles. He's too late. The locket lands in the whirlpool with a *splash!*

"My SPELLSPRING!" he cries.

At the same time, I shout, "My heart!"

The gurgling sound grows louder. The heart starts circling. It spins around and around and around, creeping towards the white light, which is still shrinking

– except not fast enough. My heart slips closer and closer to Death Proper…and then passes into it.

The whirlpool slows. Stops altogether.

The porthole seals shut.

CHAPTER 26

I would have thought that watching my heart get swallowed up by Death Proper would hurt more. Or at least, that it would hurt a little bit. But nope, I don't feel a thing.

The same can't be said for Worst-Witch.

"WRETCHED SPIDER!" he cries.

I struggle against the ropes that are tying me in place. I twist and pull but I can't move. And so, there's nothing I can do except watch as Worst-Witch's free hand – the other one clutches the banshee-in-a-bottle – comes alive with a glittering cloud of acid green, which then twists to form a thin cord. And that cord snakes along Worst-Witch's wrist.

"Simon!" I shout. "Look out!"

But Simon doesn't turn and run.

Instead, he launches himself right at Worst-Witch.

At the same moment, the Witch releases his spell. The green smoke shoots away from him, knitting itself into a net in the air. It catches Simon beneath it, trapping him. "You will pay for losing my locket," Worst-Witch snarls. He raises his free hand again. Darkness gathers around it, and he begins to mutter some curse. But then –

SKWEEE-oargh!

– the weresquid crashes back through the door.

They shoulder Worst-Witch to the floor and the gathering magic dissolves into nothing. The banshee-in-a-bottle spins in the air as if in slow motion. All eyes – fourteen of them, eight belonging to Simon – watch on helplessly as it falls, falls, falls…

…and then shatters on the floor.

There's an explosion like a hundred fireworks – *BANG! POP! BANG! BANG! POP!* – in all of the colours of the rainbow. Plumes of purple smoke erupt from the remains of the Woeful Ware, as the fireworks reorder themselves into the shape of a ghost.

A ghost with skinny arms and legs.

Springy hair. Eyes like topaz.

"GIRL!" I cry.

Worst-Witch magics another cloud of green smoke. He shoots it straight at the weresquid. As it did with Simon, the smoke turns into a net before it strikes them –

SKWEEE-oargh!

– and now the weresquid is trapped, too.

A shuffling sound tells me that Gorflunk and Scraggleknee have stumbled back into the room, grumbling and groaning between themselves. When they move into view, I see why. Their robes and seal furs are torn and tattered. Their hair is all over the place. Both Witches are still untangling themselves from their bindings, muttering about revenge.

"What did we missssss?" says Gorflunk.

Scraggleknee eyes the shards of glass covering the floor. He looks towards Worst-Witch, eyes wide.

"Master," he says. "Scraggleknee can't help but notice...the locket."

Worst-Witch glares at both of them and doesn't say anything.

"Do you have a plan?" whispers a little voice beside me.

"You're okay!" I say to Girl, relieved.

"I'm fine," she laughs. "But Corpse, do you have a *plan*?"

I look down at my rope bindings. "No."

There's only one spell I can think of that will help us now – a spell that both Girl and I have had used against us – but I don't know the words to it. And even if I did, I'm not sure I have enough magic left in me to manage it. "Well, I have *half* a plan," I tell Girl. "But I can't do anything without *Magikal Maledictions*. Or while I'm tied up."

I explain what I'm thinking to Girl.

Beyond her, Worst-Witch is stalking towards me. Over his shoulder, I can see Simon and the weresquid struggling beneath their nets. Gorflunk and Scraggleknee take their places behind Worst-Witch and follow him to where I am – stuck here on the bench.

Girl eyes Worst-Witch. "There is *one* way you could do that spell."

Realizing what Girl is suggesting, I say, "But I thought that—"

"Do you reckon you can do it?" she interrupts.

"*Maybe,*" I say.

(Really, though, I have no idea.)

"I *know* that you can," she tells me and smiles.

"But you said that—"

"Forget what I said. This is different."

The Witches stop at the concoction bench, all three of them leering down at me. "You have stepped in the way of our plans too many times tonight, wax ghost," Worst-Witch rasps, reaching into his pocket to retrieve the very last of his malicewater. There's still half a vial left – more than enough for the three of them – but he unstoppers it...

...and downs it all in one gulp.

"Masssster," Gorflunk says. "Forgive me, but isss it advisssable to consssume ssso much at once? We have no more. And without the Ssspellssspring—"

"Silence!" Worst-Witch orders.

His ember eyes glow brighter than ever.

They look like flames, buried deep in ashen sockets.

"I want no shortage of magic," he says, "for what I'm about to do."

Worst-Witch steps closer to me. His whole body is shaking. I don't know whether it's from the huge dose of malicewater, or if the thing he's brimming with is rage. He leans down, grey teeth gnashing. There are little flecks of spit all over his chin. "Can you feel pain, wax ghost?" he asks me, before raising one hand. "I really do hope so."

Worst-Witch murmurs a spell…

…but not much seems to happen. As far as I can tell, the only thing that changes when he says the magic words is that his fingertip turns all blackened and charred. The veins that run down his arm and under the skin of his hand swell and become purple – all of them feeding his fingertip with whatever dark magic he just summoned.

"Do it now!" Girl urges me.

Before I get a chance to do anything, Worst-Witch

presses his long and crooked finger against my arm, and my whole body feels like it's going to erupt into flames. Searing, scorching pain ripples through me in shuddering waves. And at the same moment, the ropes around me begin to constrict. I writhe against them, and they respond by squeezing tight.

But then, and just like that…

…the pain vanishes.

Worst-Witch says, "Very good."

I look down at my arm, expecting it to have melted right off, but it's completely fine – except for a round and charred mark where Worst-Witch touched it.

"You have cost me everything tonight, ghost," he says.

Scraggleknee watches hungrily through bloodshot eyes. Gorflunk too, except through glowing purple ones. From the corner, I hear a worried *click-click-click*.

Girl says, "*Hurry*, Corpse! Do it now!"

And so, I do.

My abalone shell eyes lock on Worst-Witch, and I try to imagine what life must look like to a person so horrible. To someone so twisted and evil and cruel.

As I imagine it, he turns kind of glassy-eyed.

His hand drops to his side.

Some invisible connection springs to life – a sort of corridor between me and Worst-Witch – and soon, it's like I'm seeing two versions of the same moment at once. Two versions of the shack at once. It's almost like I have double vision or something. I can still see Worst-Witch's face looking down at me, with the ceiling behind him. But I can also see my *own* face, too, resting against the concoction bench and framed with a mess of seaweed. It's like I've been lifted up and out of my wax body and am now gazing back down at myself.

Or like I'm being sucked in through Worst-Witch's eyeballs.

Slowly, he fades from view completely…

…as I dig deeper into his brain.

But Worst-Witch works out what I'm doing. I feel his dusty and crumbly and rotten mind start to resist me. He shakes his head, trying to clear me from it.

"Stop that!" he says.

I come unstuck. I can tell his brain is trying to push

me out. I begin to slip backwards along the corridor that has sprung up between the two of us.

I sense it start to close.

"Get out of there!" Worst-Witch shouts, clutching the sides of his head and shaking it about, making the other two Witches stare. But I have to ignore all that, just like I have to ignore the revolting thoughts and twisted memories that litter the inside of Worst-Witch's mind. There are more of them than I could have ever imagined, but I can't afford to get distracted. I concentrate all my ghostly energies and burrow deeper.

Worst-Witch says, "Stop tha—"

And then he falls silent.

Possession is a Ghostly Act, you see.

And Ghostly Acts are different to Witch magic.

So as much as Worst-Witch might struggle against me, there's not much he can do to stop it. "I think I have a better idea for punishment," I say, and I get a shock when the words ring out in Worst-Witch's raspy voice – even though I knew it would happen.

Scraggleknee and Gorflunk look at me strangely.

(I mean, they look at *Worst-Witch* strangely.)

"Better than torture?" Scraggleknee says doubtfully.

"Do you question my judgement?" I say, hoping I sound like Worst-Witch. "*I* will decide how the wax ghost should best be punished." I turn to Gorflunk, who is as confused as Scraggleknee. "What are you waiting for?" I tell him. "Fetch me the good book."

At first, he seems like he's going to argue, but then I pull Worst-Witch's face into one of his trademark glares, and Gorflunk runs to collect *Magikal Maledictions*.

"Did you do it?" I hear Girl whisper. "Did it work?"

I give her the tiniest nod, so it won't be noticed by the Witches.

Yes, Girl, your part of the plan worked.

I just hope that mine does, too.

"Here it isss, Masssster," Gorflunk says.

And he hands me *Magikal Maledictions*.

I take a deep breath and turn away from Gorflunk and Scraggleknee, so they won't see what I'm doing. So that they won't see which page I'm hunting for in the book.

"Is...everything all right, Master?" asks Scraggleknee.

"The wax child hasss turned very ssstill," says Gorflunk.

"Never mind that," I snap like Worst-Witch.

And then I find the spell.

Somewhere in the depths of his brain, Worst-Witch – the *real* Worst-Witch – must know what I'm doing, because I feel him try to push me out again. I push back, hoping that the malicewater he guzzled just before will be strong enough to help me do the spell – and to do it *powerfully*. I begin to read the magic words. "Not wanted here, not wanted now."

Scraggleknee's eyes flick up to mine. "What are you *doing*?"

I ignore him. "It's time for you to take a bow."

"Massster," says Gorflunk. "What isss thisss?"

They look down at me – at the *wax* me, that is, lying on the bench, who up until not long ago was struggling against the ropes tying her in place, but who is now completely still, like there's nobody in there. I see the pieces fall into place in their tiny minds.

"Tricksy little ghost," says Scraggleknee.

"She hasss Posssssesssssed him," Gorflunk realizes.

My voice quivers and I hurry to step away from the other two Witches. The book nearly topples right out of my hands, but I keep going with the spell.

"Locked out for good, you disappear," I say.

Then Scraggleknee shouts, "Snatch him!"

And the two Witches launch themselves at me.

"Be far, not near. Away from here!" I finish.

I snap the book shut just as Scraggleknee and Gorflunk close their hands around my wrists. And then – they're both frozen as if time has stopped. The only things that move are their frightened eyes, which flit towards something in the centre of the room.

A tiny wisp of white fog.

Or maybe it's mist.

Whatever it is, it starts to grow. The mist or fog shapes itself into a ball, then swells outwards. It explodes.

When the mist reaches Scraggleknee –

BOING!

– it collects him up and sends him flying out the front door.

BOING!

(There goes Gorflunk, too.)

The banishment spell sends both Witches hurtling through the cave. I hear them shouting and cursing and ricocheting off walls. Eventually their cries fade completely.

It worked.

The banishment spell took them away from here. But then…

…the mist rolls over me too.

I glance at my wax body, limp and still, and realize in that second that I never thought about what might happen to *me* once the spell was done.

"Girl," I say, panicked. "I think I—"

Then the mist rips me from Worst-Witch's ancient frame. He's catapulted out the door – *BOING!* – but somehow, I stay put. I look down at the floor.

I've turned all see-through.

Bare ghost legs. Ten wriggling toes.

My Possession has come unstuck. Worst-Witch

might have been banished, but my ghostly self was left behind, without a body to protect me from Death Proper.

"Corpse," Girl says. "Is that…is that *you*?"

And then everything turns to black.

When I come to again, I'm safely back inside my little body made of wax. My hands race over my arms, up my shoulders and then down my sides, checking that everything is still in place. It is. I haven't been taken away into Death Proper. I'm still a ghost.

Phew.

Girl, Simon, and the weresquid are all watching me nervously from down by the foot of the concoction bench. When they see me moving – I'm tugging at my seaweed hair, checking it's still there – Girl beams, the weresquid smiles and Simon *click*s excitedly. He jumps up and down, and it makes the whole bench shake now that he's massive.

"I'm okay," I manage. "I didn't…you know."

Girl says, "Corpse, you did it!"

I look around.

"They're gone," she says.

The shack is a mess. The book stand has been knocked over, and the water in the fire pit is splashed all over the floor. Candles litter the place, with wax over the walls.

But Girl is right. There's no sign of the Witches.

"What happened after…how did I…?"

"Your wax body just sort of sucked you back into it," Girl explains.

I move to sit up, but my head hurts and I fall backwards again. The ropes that were tying me to the bench are gone, though, and when I look to the weresquid, I see that the ropes are hanging limply in their hands. "Thank you," I tell them. They nod and bow.

"Oh!" Girl says suddenly. "This is my friend. His name is Mister McKraken."

"Nice to meet you properly," I say to him weakly.

Then, to Girl: "Will they come back?"

She shakes her head. "Your spell was strong."

"Are you sure? What about—"

"*Trust* me," Girl says. "Take it from someone who's been banished before."

"But what if they—"

"They *aren't* coming back," Girl says. "I promise."

And relief washes through me.

Because I'm *really* tired of fighting.

Simon – who seems like he's about to explode with excitement – scuttles to my side and gives me what can only be described as the huntsman equivalent of a hug. It's bristly and prickly and not all that pleasant – but it does makes me smile. "You know, I think you might be one of the bravest spiders on the planet," I tell him once he stops.

All eight of his giant eyes look at me funny.

"Okay, fine," I say. "*The* bravest spider."

And then I actually laugh.

Chapter 27

As always, the darkest part of the night is followed by the bright light of the morning. But this time, when the sun rises over the rock-that-doesn't-exist, Girl is sitting next to me again, like she used to. Simon is on my other side, resting on his big furry spider-bum.

And Mister McKraken is here too.

The weresquid swims lazy laps of the rock, just beyond the reef. Every now and again, when he passes us by, he throws a slimy tentacle into the air and waves to us.

"I think I like him," I tell Girl.

"He's *excellent*," she informs me.

Click-click?

"Don't worry," I say. "You're excellent too, Simon."

Girl turns to him. "Oh, yes...Simon, you are *very* excellent."

I wasn't able to shrink him back to his normal size, even though I tried the un-spell a bunch of times, and so Simon still looks like a kind-of-scary, eight-legged dog. I'm not sure whether it's because *Magikal Maledictions* specifically said *not* to try the enchantment on spiders, or whether it's just because I'd never done the spell before this morning.

Either way, Simon doesn't really seem to mind.

(In fact...I think he kind of likes it.)

"It's gonna be hard to find enough flies and moths to feed you now, though," Girl says to him. "Are you sure you'll be okay, Simon, staying this big?"

Click-click-click, he replies.

"What? You're *vegan?*"

Click-click.

She beams. "Okay, seaweed it is."

The three of us sit like this for a while, watching the sun rise higher in the sky and basking in the morning light as it changes from orange to blue. The fleshies of Elston-Fright start their days early, and so already I can make out a handful of cars chugging up and down the town's streets. Between us and them, the water glitters happily, almost like the storm never happened. And even from here, I can tell that Elston-Fright has changed. The white of the houses seems a little brighter than it was yesterday, and their windows twinkle in the sunlight. I've never seen them do that before. The air is clearer now too, and I realize it's because the heavy sickness that the Witches cast across the town isn't there any more.

"The Witches must be really far away," I say to Girl.

She agrees. "I *told* you that your spell was strong."

I nod, but the thing is...I'm not exactly sure *why* it was so strong. I was only trying to banish the Witches from the rock-that-doesn't-exist. But Girl is right – my spell turned out way bigger and better than I meant it to be. Maybe it was the malicewater flowing through Worst-Witch's veins when I said the magic words, or maybe the spell was supercharged by something else completely. All I know is that it's the most powerful magic I've *ever* done.

"Corpse…Corpse, are you listening to me?"

I turn towards Girl.

(And no, I wasn't listening to her. I was too distracted thinking about magic and where it comes from. I didn't notice she was talking to me.)

I shake my head. "Hmmm…?"

"I asked what will happen once the rock fades," Girl says.

I glance back at the rock-that-doesn't-exist, which I'm pretty sure has grown even greyer and more sad-looking since I left it last night. Girl continues, "What will happen once the magic in it is gone for good? Will you still be able to do your spells, do you reckon?"

I don't answer her straight away.

Because to be honest, I don't actually know what will happen – not for sure, anyway. What I *do* know is that the thought of the Spellspring's magic running out doesn't scare me as much as it used to. "I'm pretty sure you were right," I say. "About there being other types of magic. Types that have nothing to do with Spellsprings."

Girl raises her eyebrows. "*Pretty sure*?"

Part of me wants to tell her about the house with the little blue kitchen, and about how the family that lived inside it seemed able to make magic out of nothing. Part of me wants to say that I think I might have been using that *same* kind of magic for a while now, without even realizing it. Part of me wants to explain to Girl that I'm pretty sure I stopped drawing magic from underneath the rock-that-doesn't-exist ages ago – but that I didn't know it.

I mean if I'm right about all that…

…it would explain a *lot*.

It would explain why, up in the roof I share with Simon, I never felt my magic fading, even though down below the Witches were growing weaker by the day. It would explain why last night, even *before* I was reunited with my heart, my spells worked just fine. And it would explain why the Witches and the Merchant needed a Spellspring so desperately – because none of them have magic like the family in the little blue kitchen have. Like *I* have.

But all that sounds way too soppy and so I say none of it.

Instead, I say, "There's only one way to find out."

I mutter the words for my fire hex, and straight away ribbons of flame shoot from my fingertips. They stretch out in front of me, dancing on the air. I let the ribbons wriggle away from me and move over the water, where they come to a stop just above the reef. Every time I feel them start to flicker and fade, I glance over at Girl and Simon. And every time I do, the magic in my not-chest gives two big thumps and I sense my spell grow stronger.

I grit my pebble teeth, concentrate really hard...

...and do something I've never done before.

I shape the flames into four short words.

They hang suspended in the air – but only for a second.

Then the magic fizzles out.

The words erupt into smoke.

"WHOA!" Girl says.

Her cheeks light up with happy sparkles.

Click-click-click-click-click, Simon says approvingly.

My face breaks into a smile. I can't help it. It just creeps out of nowhere and tugs at the corners of my mouth. I turn my hands over, looking at them like I'm seeing them for the first time. "*Yeah,*" I say to Girl casually. "I think I'll be all right once the rock-that-doesn't-exist runs out of magic." My grin stretches wider. I feel magic crackle and fizz and pop.

Then I say, "Let's go see what else I can do."

An hour later, we decide to take a rest. The three of us have been hunting for treasures in the tide pools. But instead of fishing through the water with my bare hands, I insisted on beckoning every single thing we found. Now, my fingers are tired from doing so much magic.

But my not-chest feels fuller than ever.

"We *still* didn't find you anything to use for ears," Girl says now, peering at the pile of shells and pebbles I dumped on the ground. "Do you wanna keep looking?"

Click, Simon says – agreeing that none of it will do.

I shake my head. "We can do that tomorrow."

"Does that mean we're staying, then?" Girl asks hopefully. "That we'll go back to haunting the roof? That things will be like they used to be?"

I think on it for a bit, then shake my head.

"Not like it used to be," I say.

Her face falls.

"It'll be *way* better this time," I promise. "We have the shack and the roof and the rock now – with zero Witches! This whole place…*all* of it is ours to haunt."

Girl's face crackles happily, and I sit down beside her.

"*And*," I say, "if we're going to stay here, I was thinking maybe it's time you chose a new name. I've been calling you 'Girl' since you arrived, but I was thinking that since we *are* going to be here for the rest of our deaths and all...you should probably pick your own name."

Girl thinks on it. Her face scrunches up.

"I like Girl," she says finally.

I smile. "So do I."

I know what I'm supposed to say next. But as easy as the words are to say when you're washed up on the bank of an estuary where nobody can hear you, it's a whole lot harder to say them straight to another ghost's face. Even *thinking* the words is enough to make my cheeks turn warm. "I'm-sorry-for-what-I-said-to-you-on-the-day-you-were-banished," I blurt out, hurrying to say it all before the wax melts off my face. Girl doesn't reply.

Not at first, anyway.

And when she *does* say something, I kind of expect her to tell me what a rubbish apology it was. She doesn't, though. Instead, she says, "I'm sorry, too, for upsetting you that day." Girl pauses. "And I'm also sorry about your heart. I'm sorry it's gone."

But I'm already shaking my head.

"It's not exactly as if it did what we thought it

would," I say. "We thought my heart was going to help me find my family and my name. But you heard the Merchant. I just turned up in Elston-Fright one day, left behind in some car. I never had a family to begin with."

Click-click-click!

Girl looks over at me and raises her eyebrows. "I agree with Simon. If you don't have any family, then what are *we* – chopped jellyfish or something?"

Warmth explodes where my tummy should be.

We spend the rest of the day cleaning out the Witches' shack.

Or at least…*I* spend it cleaning the shack.

Simon tries to help, but eight legs mean that he's not much use, and eventually he decides to take a nap in the corner instead. Girl doesn't even bother pretending like she's going to help. "I don't have a body," she reminds me, conveniently ignoring the wardrobe full of Witches' clothes she could Spook. "I don't reckon I'd be much good at cleaning."

Instead, she sits on the concoction bench, announces that her skills are best put to use in a supervisory role, and then spends the afternoon giving me instructions. Or asking questions like, "Don't you reckon dolphins just look happier than sharks?" and "Do tortoises live so long because it takes them ages to get everything done?"

A smile creeps up over my face.

"What?" she says when she notices.

I shake my head. "Nothing."

She raises an eyebrow.

"It's good to have you back," I tell her.

And then she smiles widely. "It's good to *be* back."

I shake the grin from my face, then tip the book stand upright and move to empty the fire pit of water. Sitting next to it is a piece of paper, all folded up.

The Merchant's map.

It must have slipped out of Worst-Witch's robes.

Unfolding it, my abalone shell eyes scan across the town and the cemetery, then over the empty expanse of ocean below it. "You should probably draw the rock-that-doesn't-exist on it," Girl says. She's Flying now, hovering beside me and looking over my shoulder. "Maps are only useful if they've got *everything* on them."

I nod. Pocket it.

Knock-knock-knock.

The sound comes from the front door.

It's unexpected and unwelcome and I hurry to magic two snaking ribbons of fire. Just like earlier, they're powerful. They slither up and over my forearms, corkscrewing from my elbows to my wrists and awaiting my orders. Simon wakes up, bolts from his corner, and scurries over to the door. He starts clicking in a way that sounds like a growl.

Girl and I edge closer to the door.

"Who's there?" I ask.

No response.

"I *said—*"

Knock-knock.

"They can't hear you," Girl tells me. "Whoever it is...thcy'rc *alivc*."

And then she takes a step nearer.

"Who's there?" she Spooks.

I hear someone shuffling on the other side of the door.

"Whoever you are," Girl continues, "you should know that we've got a giant man-eating spider on this side of the door – and heaps of scary magic spells too!"

I direct my ribbons of fire towards the door.

"Who is it?" Girl repeats.

Eventually, a familiar voice announces, "I am the great-grandson of the last Lightkeeper. Warden of the lighthouse, guardian of Elston-Fright and protector of—"

"Flip?" I say, hurrying to snuff out my magic.

Girl looks at me, confused.

Simon *click*s.

I reach forwards and the door swings open. Framed in it is a smiling boy with silver eyes and white hair. He waves when he sees me, and then his eyes widen when they land on Simon. If anything, the sight of a giant spider makes his smile grow ever wider.

"Hi, Corpse," Flip says happily.

Chapter 28

Flip charges inside the shack without waiting for an invitation. He looks around him, face struck with something like wonder.

"Wow!" he says. "So, this is the famous Witches' shack."

Just as he did last night, Flip seems *way* too excited about something that in actual fact should probably make him afraid. He peers into each corner and squints.

"Where are they, then?" he says.

"Gone," Girl says to him. "The Witches are gone."

Then she turns to me. And when she speaks next,

I know that it's just to me. That she's no longer Spooking Flip. "You made a *fleshie* friend?" she says in disbelief. And it's not like she disapproves of the idea, exactly. If anything, she sounds kind of happy about it.

"This new Corpse really is full of surprises," she says, smiling.

"Wait, is there another ghost here?" Flip asks, spinning around.

"Over here," Girl Spooks. "I'm Girl."

He spins in the complete wrong direction and holds out a hand. "Nice to meet you. I'm Flip." Then, he pulls his hand away. "Right. A ghost. Sorry…I forgot."

Flip points at Simon. "Your spider is so cool."

Click-click comes the happy reply.

"Thanks," Girl says, "but Simon isn't ours. He's his own spider."

"Oh," Flip says, seriously now. "I understand."

"Ask him what he wants," I say to Girl. "Why is he even here?"

"I can't ask him that!" she says to me. "That's such a rude question to ask a friend." She shakes her head. "It's such a rude question to ask a friend who is a *guest*."

(If I could roll my abalone shell eyes at her, I would.)

"You know what I mean," I tell her.

"Ask me what?" says Flip. "What's a rude question?"

Girl's cheeks crackle pink. She had forgotten she was Spooking.

"It's just…" she starts. "Erm…so, Corpse and I were wondering…*Corpse* was wondering, not me. I don't mind. You can visit whenever you want. I like friends and I like visitors. But Corpse can be a bit funny about this stuff, and she was wondering—"

"Corpse wants to know why I'm here," Flip finishes.

Girl says, "If that's okay."

What follows is the strangest conversation I've had in my entire death. Without the cemetery to help me Spook him, Flip can see but not hear me. On the other hand, he can hear Girl but not see her. And although Simon has a lot to say about everything…

…only Girl and I can understand him.

Flip explains that when the sun rose this morning, he knew something was different. He says that the first thing he saw when he gazed out of his window was the rock-that-doesn't-exist – only this time, it didn't slip from his brain when he looked away again.

"Tell him it's because the Witches are gone," I say to Girl. "Tell him that the Witches' curse on the rock-that-doesn't-exist broke when they were banished."

And so, Girl does tell him. Flip nods.

"Makes sense," he says.

Flip goes on to explain that he waited all day, until his nan went to take one of her famous three-hour naps. He snuck out, stole her boat and made his way here.

("I commandeered a vessel," is how he puts it.)

"But *why* is he here?" I ask Girl.

She Spooks him again. "Corpse wants to know *why*, though."

Flip looks confused. "Because I'm descended from Lightkeepers, obviously. It's my *job* to keep an eye on all the magic stuff that goes on around here." He says the next part directly to me. "When you didn't meet me at the lighthouse, I decided to go back to the cemetery to check if you were still there. But the graves were all *open*. The whole place was a mess. I didn't know what to do until I saw the rock this morning. And then...well, then I, um—"

"It sounds to me like you came to check on a friend," Girl says.

Flip's face lights up at the word *friend*. "Yeah," he says. "Yeah...that's it!" And then Flip Little puffs his chest out and beams. "I came here to check on a friend."

When Flip tells us a while later that he has to get home, Girl looks disappointed about it. Simon *clicks* sadly. Flip makes us promise we'll visit him at the lighthouse.

On his way out of the door, the handle comes off in his hand.

He looks around at the crumbling shack.

"You really should fix this place up a bit," he says.

The four of us leave the shack and walk through the cave inside the rock-that-apparently-does-exist-now. We cross the tide pools, then Flip clambers into his nan's little yellow boat. He rips the cord and the engine sputters to life. A cloud of smoke explodes out of it and the propeller starts churning the water. The boat does a lazy circle. "You know that you've got a weresquid living just off your rock, right?" Flip calls back to us.

"He's a friend of ours," Girl says.

Flip's mouth hangs open.

"A *friend*?" he repeats.

For a moment, I think he's about to tell us how dangerous weresquids are. Instead, he says, "I'm *so* jealous. Weresquids are the coolest!"

And then he waves goodbye.

The boat starts chugging towards the lighthouse in the distance – the one that I had always thought was abandoned, but that I now know is simply sleeping. I'm glad Flip didn't mention the scally-somethings and thunder-things and polter-wotsits that he told me about last night. I guess Girl will find out about all that stuff one day, but today is not that day. We've only just got rid of the Witches. The last thing I want is for Girl to know that there's a whole world of magical terrors out there – drawn to Elston-Fright as if by a magnet.

We watch Flip and his boat shrink away in the distance.

"You know," I say, "I thought I was a goner before – when my Possession on Worst-Witch came undone. I thought Death Proper was going to be waiting to take me."

Girl shakes her head. "I reckon you're wrong about that."

"What do you mean?" I ask.

"Well…you're always saying that your wax body is what keeps you from slipping away into Death Proper, right? You always tell me that it's what ties you here. But the thing is…I don't have one, do I? And I stick around just fine. So…maybe the effi-thingy *helps* to keep you here, but I bet there's something else that keeps you around, too."

I've never thought of it like that. "Something else like what?"

(Although I'm pretty sure I know what she's talking about.)

"Probably the same thing that keeps me here," she says simply.

And it makes my not-stomach wriggle and turn warm again.

Girl suggests that we head back inside.

As we turn to head towards the rock-that-doesn't-exist, I feel the shards of the divining bone stab into my side again. I still haven't told Girl about them. I reach down and run a hand up and over them, and can't help but wonder…

…would my sticking spell be strong enough to fix it now, maybe?

"You go," I tell Girl. "There's something I want to do first."

She nods, turns away and I watch her and Simon disappear back into the rock-that-doesn't-exist's cave. Then, I take a seat right at the very edge of the tide pools and look out over the water. Without meaning to, I've found myself in nearly the exact spot where Old Man appeared out of nowhere. It's hard to believe all that happened just yesterday.

So much has changed since then.

I glance around to make sure nobody is watching, and then pull the pieces of the divining bone out to inspect them. Girl and I have barely spoken about their previous owner all day. But like the lighthouse, I guess we'll have to talk about the Merchant at some point. Because even though Girl and I haven't said it out loud, I know that neither of us have forgotten what the Merchant said. *The only person who does any snatchings around here is* me.

Which means the Merchant must have snatched Girl, too.

I turn the pieces of the divining bone over in my hand.

She was using it to hunt for the Witches, I realize. *She was hoping it would take her to them.* Only, the curse they placed on the rock-that-doesn't-exist that kept it hidden from fleshies – the curse that has broken now – must have fooled her Woeful Ware, too.

I stand up, reach into my pocket, and when I pull my hand back out again, in the centre of my palm rests the little black button – the only thing left from my life. My only clue about who I was before I became a ghost. What did the Merchant mean when she said that she *waited a very long time for the right child to arrive*? I pocket the button again and shake my head. It's just another question without an answer. And I think I've had enough of those.

I glance towards Elston-Fright.

Then, back at the rock.

Finally, I fling the divining bone pieces as far as I can throw them –

SPLASH!

– and then smile as I watch them disappear beneath the surface.

I wait until the very last ripple dies away. I wait until I'm certain the pieces are resting in peace on the ocean floor – and probably being pecked at by confused wrasse. *Sometimes things don't look the way you think they will.* The words seem to dance on the air.

"Sometimes not even answers," I mutter.

The sun is fading now, as early evening comes to steal the day's light. I turn back towards the rock-that-doesn't-exist, and I begin to make my way home. I wander across the tide pools, stopping only to run a hand over the rock, still warm from the sun. I smile at the little geckos scampering away into the cracks.

When I reach the lightning-shaped crevice, I meander through it and move deeper into the damp and familiar cave, towards the rickety and ugly shack, excited to get back to the strange little family that's waiting there for me.

Me. A kid ghost called Corpse.

Elsewhere

Somewhere far away, a father and a mother prepare for another restless night with only the sound of the rushing wind to keep them company. “How many years have I been doing this, do you think?” the mother whispers sadly, as she sets a small pillow at her side.

On it, she rests a stuffed toy.

Soft and floppy, the toy looks like a sugar glider.

All raggedy now, one of its black button eyes is missing.

A loose thread dangles from where the button used to be, and some of the toy’s stuffing pokes out from a hole behind its ear where the fabric has worn through.

But the sugar glider is a precious thing to the mother, so she carefully pokes the stuffing back inside.

"More than is fair," the father says to her.

He wraps her in an arm that has turned frail over the years.

"But someday soon," he says, "we will find our way out of this."

The mother nods – not because she believes the father, but because she wishes so badly that she did. Over the toy, she places a small silk blanket with a name embroidered in its corner. The blanket is a tiny thing. It could only ever have belonged to a baby.

"Someday, we'll find our way back to her," the father says, and again the mother pretends to agree. She knows it makes him feel better to say these words aloud each night, just as it makes her feel better to arrange the pillow and the blanket and the sugar glider.

"Goodnight, little tiger," the mother sighs to the darkness.

It's cold in the place where she sleeps, and when dreams do finally come to her, they take the shape of her usual nightmares. Each night, the same. Each night, she tosses and turns and calls out the name of the child she had to leave behind. Each night, she is returned to that day when she and the father and their baby daughter took a simple wrong turn…

…and drove into the cursed little fishing town of Elston-Fright.

WELCOME
TO THE CHARMING
TOWNSHIP OF
ELSTON-FRIGHT

Magikal
Maledictions

Acknowledgements

Firstly, to my agent, Gemma Cooper, without whom Corpse might forever have been stuck in a book-that-doesn't-exist. Thank you for the early-morning Zoom calls, the Santa hats and the important discussions about musical theatre. Most of all, though, thank you for being the very best champion for Corpse and her friends out there in the big publishing world.

To Rebecca Hill. Thank you for befriending Corpse, and for giving her a most magical home among the living. Thank you also to Anne, Alice, Beth, Fritha, Jessica and the rest of the spellbinding team at Usborne. To Maxine Lee-Mackie, for the gorgeously eerie cover, and to Eleonora Asparuhova for her wonderful internal illustrations; together, you brought Elston-Fright and its inhabitants to life. The result is a book which, simply put, is beyond my wildest dreams.

To the salespeople, booksellers and librarians whom I'm yet to meet, for helping to get this book into young readers' hands. And of course, thank you especially to all those wonderful kids who have picked up my book. I hope you had as much fun reading it as I did writing it.

Okay, now comes the part where I really start tearing up.

If this book says anything about anything, it's that friendship and family are the very best kind of magic. And so, with that in mind, I want to thank the real-world family and friends whose love and support helped make this book a reality:

Matt Saccuzzo. You were the very first fleshie to lay eyes on an early draft of *A Girl Called Corpse*. Thank you for reading it front-to-back in approximately forty-five seconds, and then for enthusiastically offering to read every single draft that came after it. Your kindness and genuine excitement for the story propped me up when things got difficult.

Tobias Madden – my friend, sounding board and writing buddy. Thank you for taking my anxious phone calls (there were a lot of them), and for encouraging me to keep writing even when it felt like maybe writing was something I was just not very good at.

Amy Tildesley. The type of friendship that Girl offers Corpse – loyal and unwavering – was inspired by watching you. Thank you for constantly reminding me what it means to be a good friend.

Magali de Castro. Hamish Barratt. Tim O'Brien. Ben Stanley. Tom Mitchell. Cam Hinkley. Ruth Hatch. All of you are, simply put, flipping magnificent people.

My family – Prue, Jake, Simon, Georgia, Martin.

And HAGGERS – the best, fluffiest and most slobbery writing companion a person could ask for.

Most importantly, thank you to Mum. For everything.

Lastly, I want to say that teachers are magical beings. Without the encouragement of one in particular – my Year Eight English teacher – I never would have thought that writing stories was a possibility for me. The faith he showed in me as a kid has been like a talisman that kept me writing all these years, and I would have given up a long time ago (or perhaps never even started) if it wasn't for him. It's no hyperbole to say that he changed my life.

So thank you, Mr Webb.

Q&A WITH REECE CARTER

Reece, there are some brilliantly spooky moments in *A Girl Called Corpse* – why do you think people love scary stories so much?

Scary stories are like rollercoasters: they get the adrenaline pumping! Reading about ghosts and witches keeps us on the edges of our seats, turning pages. And even though being scared in real life is not very much fun at all, we love scary stories because we know they are a safe place to feel those emotions. With a book, the reader is in control. If things ever get too spooky, we can just close the book for a little while and do something else! The monsters stay inside the pages.

Simon is Corpse's companion throughout the book – if you had to choose just one animal to accompany you on a quest, what would you pick and why?

I would be in big trouble if I didn't say Hagrid, my dog. He's the perfect sidekick for a quest: brave, loyal and quite possibly the happiest dog in the world. It would be impossible to feel scared with him by my side. When I think about it, Simon and Hagrid have a lot in common.

What were some of your favourite books growing up?
I loved Roald Dahl stories as a kid. They were whimsical and funny but with a deliciously dark edge. *The Witches*, *Fantastic Mr Fox* and *Matilda* were some of my favourites.

I also adored all of Paul Jennings' short story collections, like *Unreal!* and *Unbelievable!* which were turned into a television series about strange and spooky goings-on in a lighthouse (sound familiar?) called Round the Twist. When I got a little older, Neil Gaiman's books *Coraline* and *The Graveyard Book* became instant favourites.

Would you like to visit Elston-Fright? If you could, where would you go first?
No trip to Elston-Fright would be complete without a visit to the Ungeneral Store. I know for a fact it would

give me the heebie-jeebies, but I can't help it – I would love to see all those creepy magical artefacts in one place. Let's just hope the Merchant doesn't show up!

What is your best story-writing tip for budding authors?
Think big! The very best stories come from the weirdest ideas, so let your imagination run wild. If you look closely enough, inspiration lurks in the most unexpected places, so keep an eye out everywhere you go – at home or in the classroom – for your next great story idea.

If you could do one spell from Magikal Maledictions, what would you want to do?
I've always wanted to be able to turn myself invisible, and luckily, there is a cloaking glamour in Magikal Maledictions for that very purpose. It goes a little something like this:

Now you see me, now you don't;
Try to find me, but you won't.
I leave no trace, leave no trail;
Hidden here behind the veil.

What would I use it for, you're wondering? Well, that part is a secret.

Can you give us a sneak peek of what's up next in the Elston-Fright adventures?

The Witches may be banished for the time being, but as Corpse now knows, Elston-Fright has a long history of attracting bad magic. It's only a matter of time before a new evil arrives in town, and when it does, it will once again be up to Corpse and Girl to save the day.

But this time, they won't be able to do it alone. This time, magic spells and Ghostly Acts won't be enough. Along with their new friend Flip, they'll need to retrace the footsteps of the first Lightkeeper, looking for a way to save Elston-Fright before it's too late.

Look out for

THE LONELY LIGHTHOUSE OF ELSTON-FRIGHT

Coming soon...

The thing about magic is that it likes to stay hidden…

When Simon is spider-napped by an ancient magical threat, Corpse, Girl and Flip must save him. Armed only with the knowledge contained inside the Last Lightkeeper's journals, they set out to rescue their friend, but the clock is ticking.

Dark secrets come to light, as they discover that nothing in Elston-Fright is as it seems.

Reece Carter grew up on his family farm in Western Australia. There was an unfortunate lack of witches and ghosts on the farm though, and so Reece had to find them in books instead. Reece could regularly be found hiding in the library, tucked away in the corner with a good book, and with the encouragement of his English teacher, Reece started writing his own stories too. After studying health science, Reece worked as a nutritionist by day, writing for magazines and appearing on TV, but maintained a secret double life, continuing to write middle-grade novels and short stories by night. Now, Reece lives in Sydney and writes kids' fiction full-time. When not reading or writing, Reece can usually be found talking to his dog.

A Girl Called Corpse is his debut novel.

@herbnerdreece
@usborne
#AGirlCalledCorpse